Risk:

How to make decisions
in an uncertain world

Risk:

How to make decisions in an uncertain world

Editor
Zeger Degraeve
London Business School

Series Editor
Nigel Nicholson
London Business School

FORMAT
PUBLISHING

Risk:
How to make decisions in an uncertain world

Published by
Format Publishing
31 Cattle Market Street
Norwich
NR1 3DY

ISBN 1903091365

First published 2004

British Library Cataloguing in Publication data
A CIP record for this book is available from the
British Library

Series Editor
Nigel Nicholson

Editor
Zeger Degraeve

Additional editorial and writing
Tom Albrighton, Sarah Powell, Bernadette Sheehan

Cover design
Matthew Knight

Page design
Kaarin Wall

Set in Sabon and MetaPlus

Cover image
Storm clouds
by Digital Vision/Getty Images

Page images
Getty Images

Printed
In the UK by Norwich Colour Print on paper derived
from forests sustained with 'two-for-one' planting

Contents:

Introduction:

by Nigel Nicholson

In business everyone is a decision maker, and every decision maker takes risks.

For some people – fire-fighters, City traders, entrepreneurs – risk is right in the centre of their visual field, the heart of their profession. But risk is actually a central consideration in a much wider range of occupations, and in many aspects of our daily lives. Our money, our relationships, our jobs and our lives are all at risk from time to time.

The problem is that we tend not to view the world that way. Most of the time we are unaware of risks that we bear in a million everyday acts, in and out of work, and when we do think about risk, our minds are apt to fill with big and largely false imaginings. We think more about unlikely hazards, like airline crashes and threats to our organisations, than we do about traffic accidents or unexpected errors at work. We are often comfortable for others to be the risk takers whilst turning a blind eye to the risks we run. At other times, when we are confronted by challenges, we tend to have exaggerated and often inaccurate perceptions of risk.

Even experienced risk professionals – such as surgeons, bankers and business leaders – do not think straight about risk. The finest mind and the sharpest intelligence offer no protection against many of the errors and distortions that infect risk judgements, as will be illustrated in the pages that follow.

This book clears all the fog around this important topic and brings it into sharp and relevant focus for every business person. It is vital that we take risks, for otherwise we cannot achieve our ambitions. It is not an option to seek a risk-free life since that will only incur greater dangers later. Let us consider some examples.

Are you a *leader* or *people manager?* If so then you will no doubt accept that risk is always close at hand, but is it where you think it is? Is it as controlled as you would like it to be?

As a leader you will be likely to associate risks with the big strategic moves you undertake, but there are risks in many other quarters: in the key appointments you make; in the kinds of information and advice you seek when making decisions; in the calculus you deploy to quantify the costs and benefits of operations; and in your own capability to become aware of and react to the unexpected.

In this book leaders will find examples of both the large and small risk decisions that are typically confronted, how they go wrong, and how unnecessary dangers can be avoided.

Are you a *professional delivering a service?* Big risks and errors are not just in the areas that come with numbers attached to quantify the dangers. They lie in some of the least considered areas of service delivery – like entrusting a critical client interaction to a new colleague, or in drafting a report that treads a fine line in terms of what is stated or disclosed.

As we show in this book, there are many other alternatives between simply taking and avoiding a risk, strategies that allow you to take risks at controlled levels that enable you to get closest to the results you want.

Are you a *technical specialist?* Risks can often be quantified in terms of tolerances and probabilities, but these do not tell the whole story. Important risk-related processes both precede and follow risk taking, in terms of states of readiness to bear unexpected risks, and in how one judges and learns from the consequences of risk taking. Context is critical. In many highly technical worlds the risks might appear just to depend upon the immediate environment and skills of people like you, but often there are key forces at work in the surrounding business structures and cultures. The world of finance illustrates this. Norms governing the way information is processed and how errors are detected, and how managers deal with the aftermath of trading losses and gains, are all as critical as the immediate zone of action and decision.

Some parts of this book are quantitative. It is essential, wherever possible, to attach numbers to probabilities and costs within risk domains. Often the right numbers are not available, and much can be done to generate the metrics that really do reflect the risks that are important to us.

But even when presented with relevant data, even experienced professionals are apt not to use them correctly. Probability and uncertainty are poorly understood concepts and often wrongly assessed by people whom we might expect to know better.

Without getting incomprehensibly technical, in this book we aim to give laypeople and professionals alike a clear line of sight through this often-confusing numerical thicket.

But risk is not a mathematical phenomenon. It is intensely human – linked by an umbilical cord to human desires, impulses, instincts, sentiments and naïve beliefs.

We humans were not designed for precise probabilistic computation, accurate calculus and straight-line reasoning; our mental capacities are more attuned to confidence in action, self-belief, speedy intuition, focused attention, endurance and willpower. These qualities are mainly what one needs to navigate complex social networks, dare to venture into new domains, to get out of physical danger, to overcome obstacles and to keep one's clan together.

Evolution gave us a repertoire of emotions and a filter system of cognitive biases that were extremely helpful to survival and reproduction in the ancestral world of our origins as clan-dwelling nomadic hunter-gatherers.

But now we inhabit a fast-moving, highly technical world of operations, production and services that make demands on us for which we have no special capability. Our only defences in this world are our insight and corrective measures, which can help us become aware of the risks we are running and know when to seek the aid of statistical and other control systems.

These are matters of psychology, information management, leadership and culture.
The present volume encompasses all these dimensions.

It is about how we can think more clearly about risk. How we can ensure we have the right information to make risk judgement calls. How we can develop confident risk-management strategies. And it is about how we can encourage the development of organisational cultures that support risk intelligence.

1 Overview:

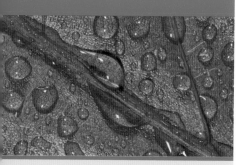

We make decisions all the time in business.

For them to lead to the outcomes we want, we need to understand the concept of risk and learn to manage it better.

Making decisions

In business, we're making decisions at every turn. Some decisions are hugely significant for the business as a whole, such as those relating to acquiring other companies, diversifying into new areas or restructuring the organisation. Other decisions have more localised consequences, such as those relating to recruiting new team members or setting work priorities for the next few months. Finally, some decisions affect mainly ourselves – such as decisions about how to organise our working day or whether to apply for a new job.

For most decisions, we know what the possible consequences are. We have a reasonable idea of the various things that could happen. Some outcomes will be good, others not so good, and some in-between. To be successful in business, we want to make decisions that lead to good outcomes.

The problem is that we don't know how likely different outcomes are. If we bring out a new product, what are the chances of success? If we invest in a new factory, how likely are we to profit from it? If we devote a day to this project, will it bring any benefit to the business?

If we need to make a decision, we often seek more information to help us. But there are no facts about the future, only probabilities. The information we obtain may well help us, but we need to remember that it relates to the past, not the future. Only in the most simple situations (such as tossing a coin) can the probabilities of future outcomes be known with certainty. In any more complex situation – and business situations can be fiendishly complex – it becomes very difficult to know the chances of a good outcome. In other words, risk is involved.

We deal with risks every day, in life and in business, often without stopping to think about them in any detail. The concepts are complex and can be hard to understand at first sight, making it tempting to neglect them. But we need to get to grips with them, because although we may feel confident about our decisions (for reasons we'll look at later), the reality is that we are very poor at calculating probabilities and assessing impacts. Moreover, our decisions are much more deeply affected by our personalities than we might like to think. In our personal lives, the results of poor decisions may be negative, but we are the only ones affected. In business, there may be far-reaching consequences.

This book will help you get to grips with this by improving your understanding of risks and learning new, more effective ways of making decisions – and dealing with their consequences.

Risky situations

Any time we face a decision in business, we are dealing with risk. Some typical situations where we face risks include:

- [ ] **people:** recruiting new staff; creating teams and departments; promotions; recognition and reward

- [ ] **strategy:** decisions about expansion; moving into new business areas; acquisitions and mergers

- [ ] **resources:** decisions on outsourcing and re-allocating resources within the business; investment decisions

- [ ] **processes:** decisions on the way the business works; setting operational procedures; health and safety policy

- [ ] **managing projects:** alternatives for different approaches; the implication of timescales and resources; potential problems endangering delivery.

Introduced in February 2003, Mayor Ken Livingstone's bold and controversial congestion charging scheme for central London illustrates several of the key concepts of risk and decision making that we will examine in this book.

The decision to introduce the scheme had several dimensions of risk:

- ☐ **financial:** the scheme needed to bring in revenue for the City; the costs of implementing it were high

- ☐ **operational:** the project was innovative and there was uncertainty over whether the systems involved would actually work

- ☐ **reputational:** Ken Livingstone was strongly identified as the architect of the scheme; failure would have jeopardised his personal reputation and public standing as mayor.

So, what made this risk worth taking? There were several potential positive impacts:

- ☐ **improved conditions** for London drivers and pedestrians

- ☐ money to spend on **public transport improvements**

Risk is present whether or not we understand that we face a decision. In some situations, it will be very clear that a decision is required – at the outset of a project, for example. In others, it may not immediately be clear. It's possible that many aspects of your business could be improved and that a decision needs to be made, but no one has realised it yet. However, the risk of continuing along your present course is real.

Upsides and downsides

The word 'risk' has strong overtones of danger, and indeed it is generally 'downside risk', or reducing the probability of loss, that is the focus of risk management. We are often more concerned with avoiding mistakes than we are with securing success.

However, risk doesn't always mean danger; many decisions also have

- [ ] **environmental** improvements
- [ ] a **personal victory** for the city's first mayor in modern times.

As we shall see, taking risks to secure positive outcomes depends on sharing information and building commitment to joint decisions. But winning the hearts and minds of Londoners to this ground-breaking scheme was never going to be easy. There was disagreement over its likely impacts:

- [ ] negative **individual impacts:** Londoners didn't like the idea of paying to drive in their city, regarding public transport as a poor alternative
- [ ] negative **business impacts:** retail chains feared a marked decline in trading.

In the early days, media coverage was often unfavourable. One reason for this was the unreliability of probability information. Estimates of income proved over-optimistic; the probability of reaping large financial rewards had been overestimated. There was also a short-term negative reputational impact: the company tasked with administering the scheme had a rocky start and Livingstone was blamed for rushing in the scheme.

Yet within a year of its introduction, the positive impacts of congestion charging seemed to outweigh the negatives. It was being widely seen as a success, and plans were announced to extend charging westwards. Car usage was estimated to have declined by 30%, and other cities were considering launching similar schemes. Ken Livingstone's reputational risk also paid off: he was accepted back into the Labour Party from which he had been expelled in 2000 when he stood as an independent mayoral candidate.

a potential upside. And, as we shall see, even the worst 'bad' outcomes have one very important upside – they allow us to learn from our mistakes.

In business, taking risks is often the only way to realise opportunities for growth and innovation. Caution locks us into established ways of doing things, and this is a risk in itself if it doesn't secure the long-term future of the business.

Decisions that look 'adventurous' or 'risky' may actually be aimed at reducing the long-term risks faced by a business. 'Doing nothing' or continuing on your present course is a choice as well – and it's not necessarily the right one.

So, when we talk about risk, we mean the information and analysis that goes into making difficult business decisions of all types – not just those that relate to threats.

Why manage risk?

Understanding risk brings many benefits to the business. We can never be fully prepared for the challenges of the future, or ensure that every decision is perfect, but understanding risk means we can go forward armed with as much knowledge and understanding as possible. The practical benefits to the business of understanding risk include:

- **preparing for problems** before they affect the business (rather than reacting afterwards)

- ensuring **business continuity** when problems do occur

- **improving** operations, systems, processes and management

- **reducing costs** (or simply understanding where and why they are incurred)

- **demonstrating** the soundness of your chosen approach to others (perhaps those outside the business).

Building up an understanding of risk also helps you to improve the way you make decisions. This has bigger benefits for the business than practical or operational improvements.

A business secures its future through the quality of the decisions it makes about what it will do in the future. Good decision makers are those with skills that include:

- backing up decisions with **information** wherever possible

- **explaining** situations and decisions more effectively to others, to build a shared perspective on issues facing the business

- **justifying** decisions with real information and sound reasoning, not just common sense or instinct

- building up **awareness of the opportunities** (as well as the threats) that are present in every business situation

- creating new **alternatives** for every decision, to ensure that every alternative is considered before a decision is made

- building a **consensus** that is based on shared understanding and perspectives

- **understanding how decisions are taken**, particularly the way values, bias and past experience can distort objectivity; learning to overcome this as far as possible.

About this book

The rest of this book looks at the following areas, which help us to make better decisions when risk is involved:

- **types of risk:** the areas of the business where risk comes into play in decision making (chapter 2)

- **probability and impact:** how likely it is that different outcomes will occur; the impact on the business if they do (chapter 3)

- **tools:** the methods we can use to structure and analyse decisions (chapter 3)

- **responses:** different tactics we can use to respond to risks if we can't avoid them (chapter 4)

- **risk psychology:** what effects our own characters and values have on the quality of our decision making (chapter 5)

- **learning:** how we can turn 'bad' outcomes into good ones by learning from our mistakes when things go wrong (chapter 6).

Looking back:

Key ideas from this chapter

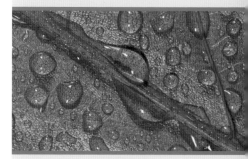

- In business, we are making decisions all the time, whether we are aware of it or not.

- We need information to help us make decisions, but there is no information about the future – only possible outcomes and different probabilities.

- Measuring risk helps us get to grips with uncertainty by understanding the probability and impact of different possible outcomes.

- It also helps us prepare for the future and learn more about the way in which we make decisions.

2 Types of risk:

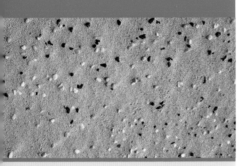

Risks can be divided into different types, based on the areas of the business they affect and their level of impact.

Understanding types of risk is useful when comparing them with one another, or building up a picture of all the risks a business faces.

Operational risks

Operational risks are problems that could arise at any time as part of normal business operation. The potential downsides of operational risks are those events or situations that would prevent or impair the business's operation if they arose.

Identifying operational risks means considering what can go wrong in the running of the business. Managing them is about being prepared for outcomes that are different from (and worse than) what we hope for – potential failures, shortfalls, mistakes and so on. Once foreseen, they are easier to make plans for. The aim of planning for operational risks is to ensure business continuity – to make sure that the business can continue without too much disruption in the event of a downside occurring. Operational risks can occur in areas such as:

☐ **people:**

  ☐ absence or resignation of key **staff** at critical times
  ☐ **errors** of judgement: failure to understand complex issues resulting in bad decisions
  ☐ **lack of key skills:** inability to carry out key tasks
  ☐ deliberate **misconduct:** fraud, theft, etc

- processes:

  - **quality control** issues
  - **health and safety** issues
  - inadequate **capacity**: failure to deal with peaks in workflow; not responding quickly enough to unusual or new demands
  - **information issues**: inaccuracy (or lack) of key information to support decision making (performance figures, for example); poor communication between individuals or teams; inadequate reporting and monitoring arrangements

- **technology/infrastructure:**

  - problems with **premises** (not large enough, not safe enough, not in the right location, etc)
  - loss of critical **data**
  - failure of key **technologies** that support the business (manufacturing, communications, transport).

Failing to anticipate and manage operational risks can be disastrous, particularly if they have the potential to affect other areas of the business. In other situations, their impact can be relatively minor.

Strategic risks

Strategic risks are those relating to the biggest decisions taken in business:

- which **customers** to appeal to; which customers not to appeal to

- which key **resources** have to come from within the business; which could (or should) come from outside it

- whether to **diversify or consolidate**

- how much to **innovate**

- whether to go for rapid **growth**

- whether to try and increase **profit or turnover** (or both), and how quickly to do so

- how to **structure** the business

- what organisational or shared **values** the business needs to adopt, rediscover or get rid of; whether it needs to find a way to renew itself from top to bottom; the kind of **culture** it needs to have

- how to shape the business's relationship with the **community** around it; its place in society; its ethics and responsibilities.

Real life : Confronting strategic risk at IBM

In the early 1990s, International Business Machines Corporation (IBM) was facing some significant strategic risks:

- **financial:** it was losing money fast and coming close to running out of cash
- **competitive:** mainframe computers and related software generated over 90% of its profits, but IBM's prices weren't competitive
- **reputational:** its corporate image was suffering because of its decline
- **cultural:** as a result of all the above, morale was very poor within the company.

In early 1993 Louis V. Gerstner Jr agreed to take over the reins as CEO. When he joined the company he was dismayed at the state of its culture, which he saw as insular and characterised by rigid structures and stultifying rules and regulations. This culture, originally a great asset to the community of IBM, had ultimately made people blind to the risks facing the business, or powerless to act against them.

Gerstner and his team set out to save IBM through a programme of transformation that involved:

- the loss of 35,000 jobs
- resisting internal pressures to break up IBM into independent, country-based units to maintain global customer focus
- reinvestment in the System/390 mainframe to the tune of $1 billion over four years, ultimately enabling price reductions
- revival of the IBM brand through a global advertising campaign and the concept of 'e-business'
- re-engineering of business processes
- changes to the culture within IBM.

Clearly, this was a painful process, and regarded by many as 'risky'. But Gerstner fully understood the strategic risks that IBM faced, and this was his considered response. His decisions illustrate the benefits of understanding strategic risks, as well as those involved in 'doing nothing' or taking a more cautious approach.

Gerstner also made his decisions on the basis of information, not the ideas of those around him. He rejected the idea that PCs would make mainframes redundant and that IBM should go with the flow, deciding instead to invest in developing server

technology. Using real information to make decisions is a key part of good decision making.

Gerstner's vision of a market-driven, customer-focused team environment signalled a major challenge for the company. The new focus required not only a huge shift in resources, systems and processes, but also in attitudes and allegiances. But it was successful. Under Gerstner's tenure IBM was restored to competitiveness, profitability and – within just a few years – to market leadership.

In the four years to 2001, high-end server revenues were $19 billion. By March 2002, when Lou Gerstner stepped down, IBM boasted world leadership in IT services, hardware, enterprise software (excluding PCs) and custom-designed, high-performance computer chips.

Read more :

Who Says Elephants Can't Dance?

by Louis V. Gerstner, Jr.

Each choice is hugely significant and brings attendant risks – not just in terms of the scale or nature of the business's everyday operations, but its future direction and continuing existence.

The potential upsides – the outcomes that the business will want to see happen as a result of dealing with strategic risks – are:

- [ ] providing for **customer needs** in a manner that secures a viable, sustainable **market position**

- [ ] **growth** in turnover and profits

- [ ] **stability,** both now and in the future

- [ ] robust and reliable business **processes**

- [ ] **management and decision-making processes** that get the best results

- [ ] optimal **use of resources**

- [ ] a strong, positive corporate **culture.**

The potential downsides of strategic decisions include:

- [ ] **competing products and services** luring customers away

- [ ] **changing customer needs** making existing products and services less attractive

- [ ] **new market entrants** threatening the business's position

- [ ] problems with **suppliers of resources,** or the prices they can offer

- [ ] problems resulting from **changes in society**: political change, new legislation, regulation or deregulation; economic trends

- [ ] implications of **new technology.**

Strategic choices are made to maximise the upsides and minimise the downsides for the business. By definition, following such choices through will involve change for the business, such as:

- [ ] developing new **products or services**; moving into new markets (perhaps internationally)

- [ ] **acquiring** other businesses

- [ ] re-allocating **resources** to reflect changing strategic aims

- [ ] re-engineering or transforming **business processes**

- [ ] transforming organisational **structures**; recruitment; lay-offs

- [ ] taking action to alter or transform the **culture** of the business.

Managing strategically is about making decisions that maximise upside risk, and minimise downside risk. Each decision leads to a change, hopefully a positive one. But inevitably, new risks will be created or simply arise over time. There will always be a new issue prompting a strategic decision.

Financial risks

Risks can have many different impacts on the business, not just financial loss – we will look at some of them in the next chapter. The main types of financial risk are:

☐ **credit risk:** uncertainty about the ability or willingness of another party to pay back money that they owe

☐ **interest-rate risk:** uncertainty about the value of fixed income obligations (such as loans or bonds) caused by fluctuating yields on similar financial products

☐ **currency risk:** uncertainty about the value of foreign currency assets caused by fluctuating currency rates

☐ **commodity risk:** uncertainty about the value of holdings in widely used commodities

☐ **liquidity risk:** uncertainty about the ability to buy or sell something quickly at its 'fair value' (e.g. business premises).

Risk has a special place in the world of finance, where it is quantified, manipulated and exploited to yield returns on investments. The nature of the game is to optimise opportunities for gain whilst controlling possible losses. The key risk term in finance is 'volatility', denoting the risk that prices or rates will change and by what degree. All markets contain volatility, but some parts are more volatile than others – emerging markets offer the riskiest opportunities, and government bonds usually the least, and it is an article of faith in finance that risk and rewards are correlated, though imperfectly. You need to speculate to accumulate.

In the finance discipline, most attention in the area of risk attaches to methods and instruments that allow risk limits to be predicted and curtailed by protective strategies. Some of the predictions come from extremely complex statistical models that tell a bank what price premium should be attached to what degree of volatility. This enables the finance house to take one or more of three kinds

Real life : Failing to manage strategic risk at ITV Digital

On 27 March 2002, ITV Digital was placed in administration. The company's collapse stemmed from an ambitious three-year £315 million deal with the Nationwide Football League to broadcast Football League games live, which foundered when ITV Digital failed to attract expected viewing numbers and advertising revenue and was unable to honour the contract. By this time only £137 million had been paid to the Football League, with £178 million outstanding. ITV Digital's attempts to renegotiate the deal were unsuccessful, and it folded.

ITV Digital started life in 1998 as ONDigital. The company was a joint venture set up by Carlton Communications and Granada, who together invested more than £800 million in it. It was renamed ITV Digital in 2001. At that time, it was the only British terrestrial digital television broadcaster, and the most costly digital terrestrial television venture in the world.

The UK government was actively promoting digital terrestrial television, its Digital Action Plan envisaging a switchover to this medium by 2010. Carlton and Granada were granted a 'digital dividend' – a rebate on the tax levy on their analogue Channel 3 licences for subscribing households. This rebate, according to government reckoning, was worth tens of millions of pounds. By 2002, digital TV was being received by almost 40% of UK households.

So, what went wrong? One huge strategic risk was posed by uncertainty over customer numbers. The success of ITV Digital depended on the number of customers it could attract. Carlton and Granada expected ITV Digital to have 2 million subscribers by 2002 – a figure that turned out to be wildly optimistic. (In defence of ITV Digital, the Independent Television Commission (ITC) and Radio Communications Agency have been blamed for assuring ITV Digital that the power of its broadcasting signal would be increased. In the event, reception in large areas of the country was poor, significantly limiting the company's coverage.)

This critical failure to manage a strategic risk was compounded by a failure to manage business and operational risks:

- **cashflow:** the company had a crippling cost base (it was, for example, subsidising each set-top box given away to the tune of around £230); advertising revenue was lower than expected; the football deal came to be unaffordable

- **skills:** insufficient in-house skills to succeed in the pay-TV market and failure to seek help from outside experts

- **technical issues:** set-top boxes had insufficient memory, leading to constant crashes

- **a culture of conflict and blame:** constant clashes between the bosses of Carlton and Granada, Michael Green and Charles Allen, over investment in and visions of the company; conflict within ITV Digital, leading to the departure of several members of the senior management team.

of protective measures: 'hedging' (see chapter 4), various kinds of insurance, and proactively managing assets and liabilities to cover for possible cash flows and shocks. But any and all of these measures can let you down when reality goes beyond the parameters of the models being used to predict costs and outcomes. This is what happened in the notorious case of Long Term Capital Management (LTCM), a prosperous hedge fund that collapsed in 1998 when a global liquidity crisis pushed the real world beyond the predicted limits of the sophisticated models being used. LTCM's chagrin was compounded by the fact that it numbered on its board the Nobel prize-winning economists whose model it had been relying upon.

Project risks

We can define a project as a piece of work that is bounded in scope and/or time, designed to achieve specified outcomes or produce specific deliverables. Project risks (also known as 'issues') are potential problems associated with a particular project that could endanger its success.

The key activities to deal with project risks (identification, analysis and management) are likely to be carried out in a relatively short timeframe. The impacts of project risks are typically confined to the project itself, rather than affecting the business as a whole. It's often useful to distinguish between cost, quality and time impacts on a project – three interrelated types of impact that often have a significant effect on its success.

Managing project risks is a highly specialised subject, which we will not look at in detail here. But the techniques for dealing with risks outlined in the following chapters are generic and could be applied to project risks.

Read more :
Project Management in Practice
by Samuel Mantel, Jack Meredith, Scott Shafer and Margaret Sutton

Dependencies and knock-on effects

Risks rarely have isolated, bounded consequences. Assessing the impact of risks is often made more difficult by the fact that their effects are not localised. This makes them more difficult to get to grips with.
It also means that the implications of managing a single risk 'spill over' into the analysis or management of other risks, making the task of risk management much more complex.

Knock-on effects, or interdependencies, associated with risks can include the following:

- if one risk occurs, another risk becomes more likely to occur

- if one risk occurs, the impact of another risk becomes more severe

- the cumulative impact of different risks occurring is more significant than if they had occurred separately.

Essentially, risks need to be managed together, or jointly, when they have interdependencies with one another. While this is simple in theory, problems arise when the risks are in different parts of the business, or they are of different types. The respective 'owners' of each risk may not be aware of the potential consequences of 'their' risks occurring at the same time as other people's.

Some hugely significant disasters, such as those at Bhopal and Chernobyl, have been caused by a range of different factors going out of tolerance simultaneously. Insignificant in themselves, their occurrence at the same time proved catastrophic. This illustrates the importance of developing a system-wide approach to risk, rather than managing each risk in isolation. It may be that even though you have developed a perfect response to each individual potential problem, there is the possibility that a far bigger problem will arise if two or more risks occur at the same time.

Another dimension of knock-on effects is to move risks from one level of importance to another. For example, a single operational risk should be manageable at the operational level, but two or more may constitute a strategic risk. Individual risks within a project should be easily surmountable, and will not cause concern provided the project as a whole is still on track. But if the project is vital to the business, the possibility of many project risks occurring will need to be managed as a strategic risk.

As a result of all this, it is important to decide when risks will be escalated to the next level of responsibility; that is, when a risk will present a potential downside of such significance that it needs to be managed at the strategic rather than the operational level.

Looking back:

Key ideas from this chapter

- [ ] Operational risks are those relating to the continuity of the business's operations and processes.

- [ ] Strategic risks are those relating to the long-term survival, stability and growth of the business.

- [ ] Financial risks relate to the possibility of upsides and downsides that are purely financial.

- [ ] Project risks relate to bounded areas of work oriented towards specific goals.

- [ ] Risks of different types can have dependent impacts, or have the potential to combine and form a risk of greater significance.

3 Understanding risk:

As we have seen, most business decisions involve risk, and to deal with it we need to understand our decisions in as much depth as possible.

This means getting to grips with the concepts of probability and impact, which is the focus of this chapter.

Probability

To manage risk, we have to be able to measure it, and to measure risk we have to use probability. Probability is the quantitative language of risk and uncertainty.

The probability of an outcome is a number expressing the likelihood of it actually happening. It can be a number between 0 and 1, where 0 indicates an impossible outcome and 1 a certain one, or it can be expressed as a percentage (a number between 0 and 100).

In some situations, probability is objective and factual. For example, the probability of calling the toss of a coin correctly is 0.5 or 50%. However, tossing a coin is a very simple event. It is easy to use past experience and real-world knowledge to assess the probability of a 'heads' or 'tails' outcome. As situations become more complex, it becomes progressively more difficult to be objective about probabilities; they become more subjective. Business situations are extremely complex, and therefore the probabilities involved are highly subjective.

Because the decisions we make in business are so important, it is vital to try and pin down the probabilities involved, even though it may be impossible to achieve complete objectivity. The more precision we can bring to the situation, the firmer the foundation on which we make a decision. To move towards precision, we need to look at subjective probabilities.

Subjective probabilities

Subjective probabilities are an unavoidable part of business decision making. The following fictional example illustrates what this means for business people.

Peter and Paul are writing a report for shareholders on the strategic issues facing their business. One of the sections sets out the five-year plan for the business, including its planned response to possible future deregulation, which could have a big impact on the industry in which it operates.

The situation is very complex. The present government is planning the deregulation, but may not be in power by the time the plans come to fruition. Various individuals in government have different views, and may not reach agreement. On top of that, industry leaders are making their views felt in the corridors of power, and this may have an impact.

All this complexity doesn't prevent Peter and Paul from forming a view – maybe nothing more than an instinct or a hunch – that deregulation is going to happen. Perhaps they agree that it is 'quite likely' that regulations governing their industry will be repealed in the next two years. Since this is of strategic significance to the business, it has to go in the report.

But as they actually put their thoughts down on paper, they might stop at the phrase 'quite likely' – after all, what exactly does it mean? Peter may think it means 'almost certain', while Paul considers it means 'fifty-fifty'. In other words, Peter thinks 'quite likely' equals a probability of (say) around 95%, while Paul assumes it denotes a probability of around 50%.

To bring their views closer together, they could use a probability that is objectively knowable – such as the throw of a dice – for comparison. Do they think deregulation is more or less likely than throwing a six? If less, the probability is lower than 1 in 6 (0.166). If more, the probability is higher. By discussing the issue in these terms, Peter and Paul can move closer to a picture of probability that they both share – and one that they can communicate to others with some degree of confidence. They will also use information to help them pin down this probability – combined with their own opinions, experience and intuition. Let's say Peter and Paul agree on a probability of 75% that deregulation will occur within the next two years.

It's important to note that, just because two people have agreed a figure, the probability hasn't become any less subjective. Using numbers adds clarity and precision but does not necessary indicate accuracy. In the report, Peter and Paul will need to explain the facts and reasoning behind their probability calculation, and stress the fact that the probability remains subjective even though it has been expressed numerically. (They might use a range, such as '70–80%'.)

Some decision makers may regard this as pointless – how can that help you make a decision? If you can't know probability objectively, why waste time trying to quantify it? The answer is that it doesn't help you make the decision, but it does focus attention on the objective basis (if any) for assessments of probability. It forces you to bring your information, reasoning and judgements into the open, so that others can see them.

In the example, Peter and Paul are forced to reach a shared understanding of probability so that they can communicate it to others in their report. While this doesn't necessarily make it easier for them to make strategic decisions, it does mean that whatever decision they take will be based on the facts that are available – or draw attention to the need for more facts. Expressing probability numerically is also likely to focus everyone's minds on the urgency of the issue, rather than letting them adopt whatever interpretation of 'quite likely' suits their own values and priorities.

Another benefit is the potential for sensitivity analysis: to assess how the impact of a particular risk changes with respect to changes in probability. Bigger changes mean higher sensitivity.

Impact

Probability is the likelihood that a particular outcome will occur. Impact is the effect that a particular outcome will have if it does occur.

Impacts can be positive or negative. We call positive impacts 'upsides' and negative impacts 'downsides'. A single decision may involve the potential for both upsides and downsides.

Considering impact helps us weigh up different possible outcomes against each other, to assess how bad they will be for the business (if they are downsides), or how much benefit they will realise (if they are upsides).

We can think of impacts as 'hard' and 'soft'. 'Hard' impacts affect areas of the business such as:

- [ ] **financial:** losing or making money; changing profit margins; changes in share price

- [ ] **performance:** changes in turnover; changes in business volumes; problems with quality, or improvements; losing or gaining customers; growing the business or seeing it decline

- [ ] **business continuity:** whether business operations can continue when problems arise; whether new demands, or peaks in demand, can be met; the availability of business-critical systems

- [ ] **individuals and groups:** physical safety; financial status and reward; working conditions; workload; level of responsibility; status and authority; prospects for the future.

'Soft' impacts affect areas of the business including:

- [ ] **reputation and brand equity:** how the business, its products or services and its actions in society are perceived in the wider world

- [ ] **morale and motivation:** how people feel about working for the business

- [ ] **faith in management:** whether people believe in management's abilities and vision for the future

- [ ] **sense of community:** whether people identify with the business and its aims and feel part of the business's culture

- [ ] **social standing:** people's sense of value or relevance to the business; their sense of authority or power.

Real life : Warren Buffett's Midas touch

The golden touch of Warren Buffett in the stock market is legendary. Annual general meetings of his enormously successful Berkshire Hathaway investment company typically attract thousands of investors hoping to learn something from the mouth of the master or, even better, that something of his success might rub off on them – during 2003, Buffett oversaw a gain in net worth of $13 billion.

The decisions that have made Buffett the second wealthiest man in the world have included investments in Coca-Cola, American Express, Gillette, *The Washington Post* and Wells Fargo, plus some major acquisitions in the fields of insurance, house building and building materials, clothing and furniture. During 2003 Buffett, contrary to some market expectations, engaged in currency speculation against the dollar. By the end of the year his company held some $12 billion in foreign currency.

Buffett's success is founded on information. When, during the 1990s, undervalued stocks were becoming more difficult to find, Buffett turned his attention to corporate acquisitions. His next field of

operation, in 2002, was junk bonds – until prices rose. The subsequent foreign currency operation built on the US trade deficit when foreign investors were flooded with dollars.

Buffett takes a long-term view and typically shuns debt. During the dotcom boom he preferred to steer clear of high-tech stocks, his attitude appearing old-fashioned to many. In the event, his preference for more traditional

and easily understood firms and products bore fruit. He had correctly gauged the low probability of dotcom stocks rising. He likes to ask 'disconfirming questions' (see chapter 5) to avoid biased decision making.

Buffett also understands the need to avoid fatal downsides. He has said that he has 'never believed in risking what my family and friends have and need in order to pursue what they don't have and don't need'.

Subjectivity and impacts

The problem of achieving objectivity applies just as much to assessing impacts as it does to gauging probabilities. It can be difficult to establish a basis for comparison, particularly in the area of 'soft' impacts. As with probabilities, the key is to express impacts numerically. The commonest way to do this is in financial terms.

'Hard' impacts often lend themselves to quantification and comparison, making it relatively easy to express them financially. For example, an interruption to the operation of a production line resulting from a power cut could be translated into likely impact on revenues or profits.

'Soft' impacts are much more difficult to quantify, but they can still be hugely significant for the business. For example, falling revenues may result in disillusionment within the business – a negative cultural impact. This may result in talented individuals leaving the business, which could lead to a self-perpetuating cycle of decline (a strategic risk). Quantifying impacts financially helps to express the significance of 'soft' impacts in terms that everyone can understand, putting them on the same basis of credibility as 'hard' impacts.

As with probabilities, complexity also adds to subjectivity:

- ☐ **range of impacts:** impacts can affect many different areas of the business, making it hard to gauge the total impact

- ☐ **interdependencies:** one impact may result in another impact in a different area of the business

- ☐ **lack of precedent:** the situation may be unprecedented, or the precedent may be far in the past, making it difficult to assess the likely impact today.

Decision trees

To see how probability and impact relate to each other, we can use the simple example of a dice game. In this game, you bet £1 on the throw of a dice. Throwing a six wins a prize; throwing any other number means you lose your £1.

In version A of this game, a bet costs £1, but you can win £10. The diagram below represents the decision about whether to play version A as a 'decision tree'. Decision trees represent different alternatives and the outcomes associated with each as 'branches', to help in decision making.

Decision tree for dice game version A:

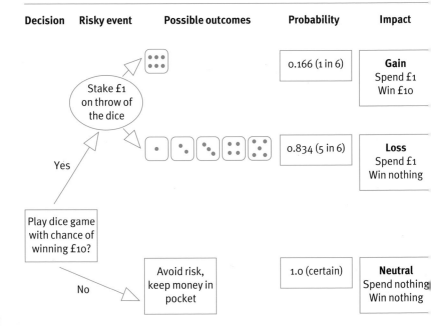

Decision	Risky event	Possible outcomes	Probability	Impact
	Stake £1 on throw of the dice	(six)	0.166 (1 in 6)	**Gain** Spend £1 Win £10
		(1,2,3,4,5)	0.834 (5 in 6)	**Loss** Spend £1 Win nothing
Play dice game with chance of winning £10? — Yes				
— No		Avoid risk, keep money in pocket	1.0 (certain)	**Neutral** Spend nothing Win nothing

Faced with this game, you have two alternatives – to play or not to play. Once playing, there is nothing you can do to affect the outcome – so your decision on whether to play has to be made on the basis of the probabilities and impacts involved. They have been entered on the tree to help your decision.

Because the situation is simple, the probabilities of the various possible outcomes can be objectively known. There is no subjectivity over the probabilities. The impacts, too, are fixed and clearly set out by the rules of the game (the prizes and the cost of playing). If a choice is made to play, the probability of winning is 1 in 6 (0.166 or 16.6%) and the probability of losing 5 in 6 (0.834 or 83.4%). If a choice is made not to play, risk is avoided (there is a single outcome that is certain) but there is also no potential benefit.

Expected value

Let's look at another version of the dice game: version B, shown as a decision tree on the second diagram below. In this game, the stake and odds remain the same, but you can only win £5. The alternative not to play remains.

Decision tree for dice game version B:

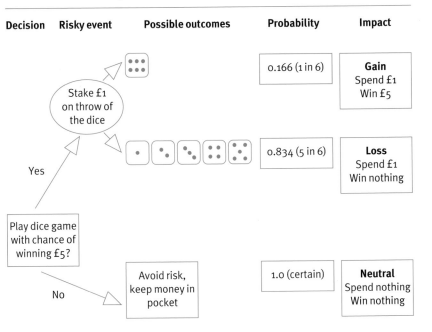

Decision	Risky event	Possible outcomes	Probability	Impact
	Stake £1 on throw of the dice		0.166 (1 in 6)	**Gain** Spend £1 Win £5
Yes			0.834 (5 in 6)	**Loss** Spend £1 Win nothing
Play dice game with chance of winning £5?				
No		Avoid risk, keep money in pocket	1.0 (certain)	**Neutral** Spend nothing Win nothing

In each case, we have to decide whether to play or not. There is the alternative to walk away, but this offers no benefit. Is it better to play, or not to play? Version A seems better than version B, but how much better? Is B worth playing as well, despite the lower prize? How can we make a decision about where to make an investment? Most people can offer answers to these questions based on an intuitive, subjective grasp of probability and impact. We make decisions all the time on this basis. But for business decisions, as we've seen, we need to move beyond subjectivity whenever we can. We need to quantify things wherever possible.

To compare different alternatives against each other in a quantitative way in order to determine whether a risk is worth taking, we can use the concept of expected value (EV). The expected value of a risk is obtained by multiplying probability by impact for each possible outcome, and adding all the results together. If a particular impact is negative, the value for that outcome is also negative.

The table below shows the expected value calculation for playing version A of the dice game. The expected value is 0.66. Because this is a positive value, it indicates that the game is worth playing.

In version B, because of the reduced prize (a variation in impact), the picture is different. This is shown in the second table opposite. Because of the reduced prize, the expected value of version B is negative. If you play it repeatedly, you will steadily lose money over time.

In this case, the alternative not to play, although it brings no benefit, has a higher expected value (zero) than playing (−0.17). You are better off keeping your £1.

Expected value calculation for playing dice game version A:

Outcome	Impact	Probability	EV calculation
Win	Cost of playing (−£1) +£10 = +£9	0.166 (16.6%)	1.494
Lose	Cost of playing = −£1	0.834 (83.4%)	−0.834
Expected value			**0.66**

Expected value helps us ascertain whether a particular alternative is worth taking, based on our knowledge of probabilities and impacts. But, unless the outcome of a decision is certain, expected value can only ever be used as a guide.

In version A, for example, the expected value of not playing is zero, and this is certain. But if you decide to play, the only possible outcomes are winning £10 or losing your £1 – in other words, values of either +9 or –1. An impact of +0.66 (the expected value) is impossible. And, while a positive expected value of 0.66 makes the game nominally 'worth playing', the outcome of playing is not certain. You might still lose.

Conversely, the negative expected value of version B, while it indicates you should not play, doesn't necessarily mean you won't win if you do. The possible outcomes are values of +£4 or –£1. You might play once and win. You might even play three times in a row and win all three times, although the probability of this is 0.0046 (or less than 1%). Despite the negative expected value, a positive outcome remains possible.

The actual probability of realising the expected value *as a result of a single decision* is zero. However, if you played version A 100 times, you would find the average value across those many decisions tending towards 0.66 – you would have around £166 in your pocket. This would prove the accuracy of your initial calculation of expected value.

Calculating or estimating expected value wrongly – or not wanting to calculate it at all – has serious consequences for decision making. Consider the National Lottery.

Expected value calculation for playing dice game version B:

Outcome	Impact	Probability	EV calculation
Win	Cost of playing (–£1) +£5 = +£4	0.166 (16.6%)	0.664
Lose	Cost of playing = –£1	0.834 (83.4%)	–0.834
Expected value			**–0.17**

Although the prize (potential upside) is enormous, the tiny probability of winning gives the game a negative expected value. But the lure of the prize outweighs the rational considerations of probability, making people mentally distort probabilities (if they consciously think in those terms at all) and decide to take an illogical risk. This is the essence of the appeal of gambling, and points the way towards the psychology of risk, which is the theme of chapter 5.

So, despite its name, we can never expect the expected value. Some may ask, in that case, why use the concept at all? The answer is to help in making decisions, rather than in predicting the future. As we've seen, there are no facts about the future, only probabilities. In this case, probabilities are known but a reliable prediction of the outcome remains impossible – the dice will decide!

We have already seen how, in most business decisions, the picture is clouded by subjectivity. Not only is it impossible to predict the future, there will also be uncertainty over impacts and probabilities.

Expected value is calculated from probability and impact information or estimates. Whatever subjectivity or imprecision is inherent in our probability and impact figures will feed through into expected values. They are only as good as the information from which they are calculated. Therefore, just as with probabilities, it is important to remember, and explain to others, when subjectivity is a factor.

Fatal downsides

Although the overall expected value of version A is positive, there is one situation in which you should not play it – when the potential downside would be fatal or disastrous for you.

If you had just £1 in your pocket, played the game once, and failed to throw a six, you would be bankrupt. The positive expected value of the game would be no help to you, since you would be unable to play any more – a fatal downside would have occurred. In other words, it is not enough just to look at the expected value of a decision. The probability of a fatal or disastrous worst-case scenario has to be considered too.

The presence of a fatal downside might temper your enthusiasm for a decision with a positive expected value, perhaps encouraging some kind of trade-off between expected value and the potential for exposure to a fatal downside. You might be better finding another dice game, perhaps a version that cost 10p to play, with a prize of 50p. This would have the advantage of allowing you to stop playing before you went bankrupt, should you hit a bad losing streak.

By doing this, you would be spreading the risk around rather than going for an 'all or nothing' risk – trading off a better risk profile for a lower expected value. (This approach to managing risk is known as 'diversifying' – we will return to it in chapter 4.)

In business terms, this translates into considering whether the downside of a risk, if it occurred, would result in bankruptcy or any situation from which the business could not recover. The possibility of this, however remote, would have to be taken into account when contemplating a risk with positive expected value.

The fact that fatal downsides in investment loom much larger for smaller companies results in the 'wealth effect' – the relative ease with which larger companies can accumulate wealth. They can take investment risks with positive expected values but serious potential downsides, because the fear of bankruptcy is more distant for them. And the more positive-value decisions they take, the more money they accumulate and the more risks they can tolerate in their investments. They can also afford to take more risks when considering and trying out new directions. Individuals can also exhibit the wealth effect: people with more cash saved up can afford to take bigger risks with their careers, perhaps allowing them to achieve greater successes.

It is the nature of known risk probabilities that the longer the run of risk taking, the closer one gets to the delivery of expected values. This is how gambling becomes a science – with deep enough pockets (the wealth effect) and enough time, pay-offs come to reflect odds. It is in the short run that 'luck' brings fortune or disaster.

Life decisions

The dice games are simple parallels with the type of decision we take every day in our lives. Investments offer the most direct comparison. With a limited sum to invest, you have to evaluate the probability of making a profit, the expected value and the risk involved for each investment alternative. And, as with the dice, you have the alternative not to play, which is 100% safe but will not make you any money.

We make other kinds of decisions too, where the investment is not always financial:

- [ ] selecting a **savings account** (which will make you richest in the long term?)

- [ ] buying a **house** (will prices fall or rise?)

- [ ] deciding which **people** to socialise with (who will turn out to be better company?)

- [ ] renting a **film** to watch (which will you enjoy the most?).

However vaguely or subconsciously, we are appraising cost, risk and expected value, with limited information about the future, all the time – even if the only cost is our leisure time, the only expected value a fleeting enjoyment, and the only potential loss a mild feeling of irritation.

A business decision

The diagram opposite shows a decision faced by a business over whether to move to larger premises, presented as a decision tree. The business estimates that there is an 70% probability that their profits will increase by 20% in the next year, perhaps because a major new customer has been found. However, their current premises will only permit them to increase profits by 10% – there is no more room for staff to do the necessary work.

Staying put does not add to costs, but preserves the ceiling on how much more profit can be made. Moving to larger premises removes this ceiling but will add to costs, effectively reducing the profits that can be made by 8%. In both cases, the probability of profit increasing is the same, since this is related to external factors (the new customer), not decisions taken within the business.

The decision tree shows that, based on the information available, it is better to stay put. The expected value of staying is greater than that of moving.

This decision tree is a good first step towards visualising a decision where risk is involved, but it has major shortcomings. Firstly, it has a narrow focus, framing the decision in terms of a single year and neglecting other alternatives such as incremental expansion and investment. Secondly, it leaves out the subjectivity that must play a part in decisions like this. How sure can we be that the probability of the profit increase is 70%?

Decision tree for moving to new premises:

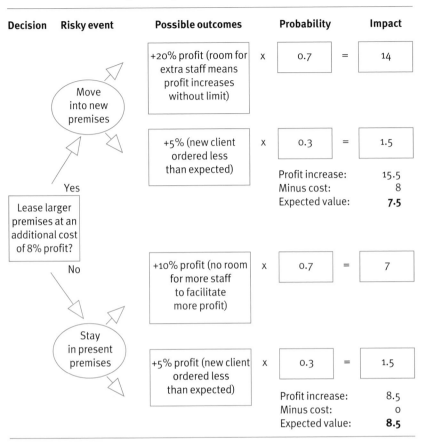

Decision	Risky event	Possible outcomes		Probability		Impact
	Move into new premises	+20% profit (room for extra staff means profit increases without limit)	x	0.7	=	14
		+5% (new client ordered less than expected)	x	0.3	=	1.5

Profit increase: 15.5
Minus cost: 8
Expected value: **7.5**

Lease larger premises at an additional cost of 8% profit?

| | Stay in present premises | +10% profit (no room for more staff to facilitate more profit) | x | 0.7 | = | 7 |
| | | +5% profit (new client ordered less than expected) | x | 0.3 | = | 1.5 |

Profit increase: 8.5
Minus cost: 0
Expected value: **8.5**

This decision tree is almost childishly simple. But simple decision trees have value because they can point the way towards more complex versions, with each iteration adding more detail and providing more understanding. Using tools like this, starting from an understanding of the essential alternatives involved, more and more knowledge can be brought to bear on crucial decisions.

Even with its limitations, this first version of the decision tree has huge value as a tool for communication; in fact, it will lose some of this value as it becomes more complex and difficult to understand. While they cannot make decisions for you, decision trees do make the underlying thinking and assumptions explicit and enable you to focus on the alternatives available, and the consequences of each.

Break-even analysis

Break-even analysis can help us to make decisions when probabilities are subjective.

The decision tree for moving premises in the previous section shows a clear-cut difference between the expected value of moving and the value of staying, demonstrating that it is better to stay than move. But this conclusion flows from the premise that the probability of the profit increase is 70%. In reality, such a probability would not be known with such accuracy. In fact, the probability might be completely subjective, a matter of intuition and judgement. But a decision must still be made.

Break-even analysis brings focus to this situation by identifying the level of probability (or any other variable) at which the decision tree is perfectly balanced because the expected value of both alternatives is the same: the 'indifference point' where neither choice is better. Having done this, you only need to make a judgement call about which side of the break-even point the variable falls to make a decision.

Let's return to the moving premises example, but use a probability of 80% that profits will increase by 20%. The diagram opposite shows the revised decision tree. Both alternatives have equal expected value, so the decision is now perfectly balanced. We therefore know that the break-even point for probability is 80%. Values lower than 80% mean that it is better to stay (we've already shown this is so for a value of 70%), and values higher than 80% mean that it is better to move. The probability remains subjective, but all we have to judge is whether it is higher or lower than 80%.

Other variables in this example could also be analysed in the same way. For example, calculating the break-even point for the cost of moving would identify the maximum that could be spent on the move without it becoming uneconomical.

The chief benefit of break-even analysis is to focus judgement calls in areas of subjectivity. Suppose the board of directors will make the decision on whether to move or not. Armed with the decision tree and break-even analysis, you could say to them: 'The decision on whether to move or not depends on how likely we are to get that big order from our new client. Would you say the chances of that are better than 80%?' If the answer is 'yes', the move should go ahead.

Break-even analysis for moving to new premises:

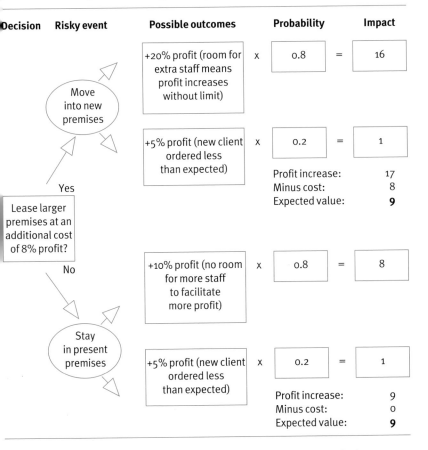

Decision	Risky event	Possible outcomes	Probability		Impact
	Move into new premises	+20% profit (room for extra staff means profit increases without limit)	x	0.8 =	16
		+5% profit (new client ordered less than expected)	x	0.2 =	1

Profit increase: 17
Minus cost: 8
Expected value: **9**

Lease larger premises at an additional cost of 8% profit?

| | Stay in present premises | +10% profit (no room for more staff to facilitate more profit) | x | 0.8 = | 8 |
| | | +5% profit (new client ordered less than expected) | x | 0.2 = | 1 |

Profit increase: 9
Minus cost: 0
Expected value: **9**

This technique would allow you to tap into their intuition and experience without drowning them in facts and figures. But at the same time, it foregrounds the fact that a decision must be made even though probability is subjective, and that success therefore rests on their understanding of the issue.

Break-even analysis can bring the values behind decisions to the fore, showing why people favour alternatives even though they are not the 'best'. For example, the board might estimate the chances of the big order at 50%, making the move 'not worthwhile'. But they might still want to move, to send a positive message to potential customers. The break-even exercise highlights the fact that this position, though understandable, is based on values rather than the benefit to the business (insofar as it is known).

Risk profiles

A risk profile is a graph showing value – usually expressed in financial terms – and probability. Looking at the profile of a risk can give a more sophisticated view of it than expected value alone.

Let's consider a third version of the dice game – version C. As before, throwing different numbers brings different outcomes. But in this version, there is the possibility of a severe downside. Throwing 5 or 6 wins £10; throwing 2, 3 or 4 wins £5; throwing 1 incurs a £10 penalty.

The different outcomes and probabilities are shown in the table below, along with the calculation of expected value for this game. As before, expected value is calculated by adding together the products of impact and probability for all possible outcomes.

At first glance, this game looks like the best so far – its expected value is far higher than that of either version A or version B. But what about the potential downside? With £5 in our pocket to play with, we could easily incur a debt that we can't pay, and have to declare ourselves bankrupt. With £20 to play with, we would be a bit safer (the wealth effect).

The key to this decision is the profile of the risk, as shown on the diagram opposite. Each vertical bar represents a possible outcome. Its position denotes its impact (negative to the left, positive to the right); its height denotes its probability. The positive side of the graph looks promising, with high probabilities for positive outcomes. But over on the left, we see the possibility of a serious negative outcome – a potentially fatal downside. The risk may have an

Expected value calculation for playing dice game version C:

Outcome	Impact	Probability	EV calculation
Throw 5 or 6	Cost of playing (–£1) +£10 = +£9	0.33 (33%)	+2.97
Throw 2, 3 or 4	Cost of playing (–£1) +£5 = +£4	0.5 (50%)	+2
Throw 1	Cost of playing (–£1) –£10 = –£11	0.166 (16.6%)	–1.826
Expected value			3.144

unacceptable profile for us, despite its positive expected value.

More complex risk profiles bring in more and more possible outcomes and probabilities. They build up a picture of complex risks and their profiles that is more useful than the simple question of whether the expected value is positive or not.

Histograms plot value against probability density, to give a continuous version of the risk's profile. They are created through advanced risk analysis involving techniques such as Monte Carlo simulations, where a large number of probabilities is used to create the risk profile.

Probability/impact matrix

Having gauged the probability and impact of a number of risks, you can use the probability/impact matrix to compare them by assessing their importance or urgency relative to one another. The diagram overleaf shows some risks that many of us face in our working lives, by way of illustration.

As with the other tools in this section, the matrix functions as a starting point for decision making. It's a good way to display or share information on a number of risks facing the business, perhaps to form

Risk profile for dice game version C:

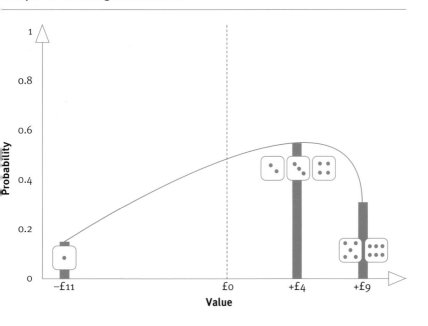

the basis for a meeting. It might be possible to compare the different risks to each other, perhaps in order to highlight situations where disproportionate effort is being put into managing a particular risk that is unlikely to occur, while another risk that is far more likely is being neglected. When risks are only expressed in verbal terms, there is a tendency to concentrate on those that sound worst rather than those that really do present the most likely or severe downside to the business. The matrix can be used to help prioritise actions, or focus efforts where they will have the most beneficial effect.

As with the other tools, in this section, it's important to remember that the probability/impact matrix is only useful in proportion to the accuracy of your own assessments of probability and impact. You only get out of it what you put in.

The information trade-off

Obtaining more information can help improve the quality of decisions by providing more detail about impacts and reducing subjectivity over probabilities. It also helps to build up awareness of other alternatives that could be taken. In general, it is a given that seeking more information will be

Probability/impact matrix:

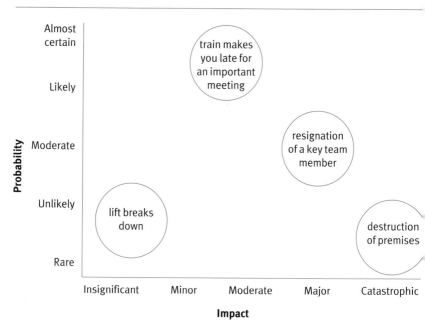

beneficial to decision makers, having the general effect of reducing the level of uncertainty involved in a decision, and making it more likely that the outcomes of particular decisions will provide opportunities for learning.

However, there is a trade-off to be made. Decisions usually have to be taken within a particular timeframe, and getting more information takes time. It can also cost money.

Both of these have implications for the level of extra effort that goes into facilitating more informed decision making.

In the case of Peter and Paul earlier in this chapter, the decision makers can reduce subjectivity by researching what is going on in government, the views of industry leaders and so on. As they learn more and more, the probability that they are assessing becomes less and less subjective. In the end (in theory at least), they can arrive at an objective probability. However, there are some important issues facing them:

☐ **getting information takes time:** Peter and Paul must write their report by the end of the month, even if they haven't pinned down the probability of deregulation

☐ **getting information costs money:** doing research will use up the resources of the business; you have to decide how much investment in information to support decision making is appropriate; this means assessing how sure you can be of the information you do have, and how much more certainty can be achieved for a reasonable cost

☐ **situations change over time:** as you collect information to help you make a decision, the context or nature of the decision may be changing; there may be a limit to the accuracy you can achieve.

Inevitably, decisions have to be made with limited information. Before you make a decision, you have to decide whether the information at your disposal is sufficient to make the decision, or whether you are going to make an investment (in terms of time or money, or both) in getting more information – and how this might affect the nature of the decision itself. (You also need to guard against the psychological traps we will examine in chapter 5.)

Management actions feed into decisions and affect their outcomes, whether this is in the form of considering decisions for longer, obtaining more information or just bringing different personal perspectives and experience to bear on the decision. There will always be uncertainty involved, but by putting time and effort into decision making, its negative effects can be minimised. In many decision situations, there is a 'third way' – the choice not to follow one of the branches on the tree, but to invest more effort in refining the picture of the decision before it is taken.

This poses interesting questions:

- [ ] how much is your time worth?

- [ ] what potential downside of this decision would you be prepared to accept if you could spend the time thinking about another issue instead?

- [ ] what potential upside do you regard as being a good 'purchase' to make with your time?

By taking the time to read this chapter, you have acquired the knowledge you need to assess whether simple games of chance are worth playing. Business decisions are much more complex and subtle than this, and you will never reach a point where you 'know everything', as in the dice game. The issue is how much time to put into making a decision, and whether to put additional resource in obtaining more information before making the decision.

In the end, this is likely to be a judgement call. While time can be quantified and given a nominal cost, the benefit to be obtained from it is likely to be very difficult to quantify. In fact, until you actually invest the time, you cannot know how beneficial the information you gain will be. We have to deal with this contradiction every time we take a business decision.

Means, not ends

Before we finish this chapter, it's worth sounding a note of caution in relation to the tools and techniques that have been covered.

However you go about making decisions, it's important to remember that people are the real decision makers. Tools and techniques such as decision trees help to generate insight into a problem, stimulate communication and build a shared understanding of it, but they cannot take the decision for you. In the last analysis, business decisions are about people – in every sense. Our favoured courses of action often flow more from our own values than from what is objectively 'right' in a situation. Our estimates of probability are similarly subjective, as we have seen. And in assessing impact, we are likely to be highly subjective too, perhaps concentrating on those areas of downside or upside that affect us most directly.

The danger of using models such as those featured in this chapter is that they can give the illusion of objectivity. Writing things down and analysing them is important, but the main benefit of doing so is to bring clarity to a decision, rather than precision.

We have to remember that tools and techniques are only as good as the information we put into them. They are dependent on the extent and accuracy of information available at the time the decision is taken. No matter how we present or analyse the information we have, we cannot add to it or make it any more reliable than it already is. All we can do is aim for a shared sense of what we know and what we don't know, to build an informed consensus for particular courses of action.

Only people can build a bridge from the information that is available to a decision that can be taken forward.

Looking back:

Key ideas from this chapter

- ☐ Probability is the likelihood of an outcome. Probabilities are expressed numerically, but are often subjective.

- ☐ Impact is the effect that a particular outcome will have.

- ☐ Decision trees help us get a grip on our alternatives.

- ☐ The concept of expected value helps us compare alternatives based on probability and impact.

- ☐ Risk profiles take us beyond expected value to consider unacceptable or fatal downsides.

- ☐ Getting more information to reduce subjectivity in decision making takes time and costs money.

4 Responding to risks:

This chapter covers the alternatives for responding to risks – the actions you can take once you've identified a risk and understood its probability and impact.

The alternatives

There are usually risks that cannot be avoided in business, no matter what alternative we choose. Our decisions therefore focus on how we will respond to them, rather than trying to avoid them. Responses to risk will vary from business to business and from risk to risk, but they tend to fall into one of these categories:

- [ ] eliminating
- [ ] tolerating
- [ ] minimising
- [ ] diversifying
- [ ] concentrating
- [ ] hedging
- [ ] transferring
- [ ] insuring.

Deciding which of these responses is appropriate in any given situation requires careful analysis of the risk in terms of probability, impact and potential outcomes.

Read more :
The Book of Risk
by Dan Borge

Eliminating risks

Clearly, if a risk has potentially negative consequences, then eliminating it is the best alternative. Given the choice, we would like to live without the potential for downsides to occur.

In business terms, this is clearly the most desirable action to take – it reduces management effort both now and in the future if you don't have to worry about a particular risk any more. However, this is seldom possible – few risks can be eliminated completely, and some risk is going to be present in nearly every business situation.

The key to considering elimination is the risk profile. As we've seen, any risk that involves a fatal downside is a strong candidate for elimination, since the occurrence of the downside, however low its probability, is totally unacceptable. We would not choose to play a dice game that might bankrupt us. In business terms this might equate to changing manufacturing processes that endangered people's lives in some way. However unlikely the outcome, it would not be acceptable simply to tolerate the risk.

Eliminating a risk may involve doing things in completely new ways. If significant business change is involved in getting rid of a risk, you may need to consider what new risks will be created as a result.

Tolerating risks

Your assessment of probability and/or impact may lead you to the conclusion that it is acceptable to tolerate a risk. Such a decision is likely to be based on one (or both) of these two perceptions:

- [ ] the **probability** of the downside is so low that it can be ignored

- [ ] the **impact** of the downside would be so insignificant that it can be ignored.

If you are satisfied that one or both of these is true, a decision to tolerate the risk may well be the right one.

By making the choice to tolerate a risk, you are basically saying that you will do whatever is necessary to recover from a downside when it occurs, but nothing to prepare for it in advance. However, this decision clearly rests on your understanding of probability and impact. If you cannot be certain of probability, you may not be on safe ground tolerating the risk of a downside.

We have seen how impacts can often be quantified in financial terms, so that they can be compared to each other. If you tolerate a risk, the business needs to be financially prepared to sustain the impact of its occurrence.

For example, if there is a risk that one in every hundred units made in a factory will be defective, but changing the manufacturing process is prohibitively expensive, the risk may be tolerated. But the business needs to be sure that the waste resulting from this decision to tolerate a risk will not damage its profits. A decision might be taken to increase the selling price of the item, or sacrifice some profit margin, to offset the cost of the risk occurring.

Minimising risks

If you choose to minimise a risk, you accept that it can't be eliminated, but take action to reduce its probability or negative impact (or both). Minimising probability means taking actions so that a negative outcome is less likely to occur; minimising impact means taking actions so that the consequences will be less severe if a negative outcome does occur.

We can see this in action by considering our own lifestyle choices. By choosing a healthy diet and exercising well, we minimise the probability of health problems in later life. By taking out health insurance, we hope to minimise the impact if they do occur. Clearly, we could do both these things – minimising both probability and impact as a result. How much action we take to minimise a risk, and the kind of actions we favour, depends on our own priorities, plus (as always) our assessment of probability and impact. If our past medical history suggested we were more at risk from health problems, we might be more motivated to take action.

A parallel from business would be typical responses to operational risks. Employees should be protected from physical harm wherever possible (minimising probability), but the employer is also obliged to have systems in place to deal with injuries should they occur (minimising impact).

Another example of minimising impact is double redundancy in computer systems. Here an entire duplicate system is created and maintained, so that it can take over in the event of malfunction. This hugely reduces the potential impact (though not the probability) of crucial data systems going offline; there is of course a trade-off in terms of cost. This is often the case: in general, the more you reduce impact, the more cost is involved. The business might choose to instate a repair contract with an IT service company instead, but this would not provide the same reduction of impact as the double-redundancy system.

Diversifying risks

Diversifying is about 'spreading risk around' – reducing your potential exposure by not having all eggs in one basket. It reduces potential negative impact, but this normally results in extra costs.

Diversification can be a good tactic where there are problems in keeping the risk 'in one place', perhaps because there is a big potential downside. For example, printers are dependent on paper suppliers to keep their operations running. By setting up many suppliers for this commodity, they make it more likely that they will be able to get cover from another supplier if one can't deliver, thus reducing the potential downside risk of running out of paper. (They also reap a number of side benefits, such as the opportunity to benchmark the prices of different suppliers, gain information about suppliers, find out about different ways of handling their orders and transactions and so on.)

However, there's always a downside. There will be more administrative work in handling a large number of suppliers, and more management decisions to be made about which one will be used in each case; is price the only factor, or is the commercial relationship important too?

Diversification is also a good strategy for managing financial risk. Investment vehicles that give investors the chance to invest in a range of companies offer those with little stock market knowledge a way to invest with reduced risk of exposure to market volatility in comparison with direct investment in a single company.

The key to diversification is keeping the different risks as separate from each other as possible, or reducing interdependencies between them. No amount of diversification will protect against a worldwide recession, but investing in different economies around the world will offset the risk of a downturn in any particular one of them.

In a project context, diversification can improve the chances of success. Suppose a project has a 0.8 (80%) probability of failure. It follows that the probability of success is 0.2 (20%) – not particularly good. Perhaps it is a speculative research and development project aimed at creating a new product.

But what if we ran two such projects? The probability of *both* failing is 0.8 x 0.8 = 0.64 (64%). And if we ran three, the probability of *all three* failing would be 0.8 x 0.8 x 0.8 = 0.512 (51.2%), making the probability of having at *least one* success nearly 50% (0.488 or 48.8%). As we add more and more projects, the chances of success in at least one case steadily increases. With 20 projects, our chances of having one success are 0.99 (99%) – we would be almost certain to succeed in one of the 20 projects. See the table below.

This illustrates how diversification can improve the chances of success, although at a price. Running 20 projects will be much more expensive than running one. But it may be that 20 modest projects, each researching a different potential product, are a better way forward than a single 'all or nothing' project putting lots of resource into a single product.

An important point to remember is that the 'winners' must pay for the 'losers' if you choose to go for diversification. The business must be able to afford to take all these risks, with all their respective potential downsides, and be confident that there is no risk of bankruptcy as a result.

Concentrating risks

Concentrating risks is the opposite of diversifying – it means

Diversifying risk through multiple projects:

Alternative	Probability of total failure	Probability of single success
Run a single project	80% (0.8)	20% (0.2)
Run two projects	64% (0.8 x 0.8)	36% (0.36)
Run three projects	51.2% (0.8 x 0.8 x 0.8)	48.8% (0.488)
Run 20 projects	1% (0.8^{20})	99% (0.99)

deliberately 'putting all your eggs in one basket'. The effect is opposite too: it increases the severity of potential impacts, but reduces management overheads, variables, unknown factors and dependencies.

An example of concentrating risk would be assigning a single person to a project full time, rather than assigning a small team part time. The time and cost of running the project might well be reduced, and the project may be run in a more coherent way, but there is a risk that the key individual will move on, damaging the chances of delivery.

The equivalent in financial terms is investing heavily in one or two stocks or products that you believe are sound, rather than spreading risk around because you are less sure of your market knowledge.

Concentrating risk depends for its success on the skill and knowledge of decision makers. With fewer chances to correct mistakes, people need to get it right first time.

Hedging risks

Hedging means taking additional risks that offset other risks, so that if the downside impact of one risk occurs, it is (in theory) balanced by the upside impact of the other risk.

An example would be betting an equal sum on both sides in a sporting fixture – whatever the outcome, you cannot lose. In investment or business, a 'perfect' hedge (one where the different outcomes are perfectly balanced) is practically impossible.

Hedging isn't just an approach to business or investment risk. We engage in many trivial hedging behaviours all the time in our everyday lives – in any situation where we wish to avoid the risk of commitment. When we hedge in everyday life, we set up alternatives for ourselves that will minimise the negative impact on us if things don't work out. Consider the planning of a Friday night out. We might make tentative plans to go out with one group of friends, but remain open to other offers. After all, a better offer might come along – with a higher probability of positive impact (more enjoyment). We are 'hedging our bets'.

Transferring risks

Transferring is the concept of placing risks with those outside the business who are best placed to manage them. Typically, this means using another company to take on a business process that you do not wish to carry out in-house, or are unable to do yourself. There are benefits in terms of reducing the probability and impact of downsides and also in-house effort in managing the risk, but there will be a cost – people will want paying for taking on risks.

Risks can be transferred in different ways:

- **formally:** on a contractual basis (e.g. IT service agreement), or through some other written agreement

- **informally:** through discussions and meetings, on a basis of trust

- **tacitly:** through assumption, perhaps based on precedent or simply beliefs.

Tacit risk transfer is generally not beneficial – it often represents a situation where one party has wrongly assumed that the other one will take an action or respond to a situation. To prevent problems like this, you need share all information on the risk with the potential transferee: its nature, probability and likely impact (on both parties); what you will pay them to take it on, why you want to transfer it and so on.

Payment for taking on risks will be most realistic when there is frank and realistic discussion of probabilities, impacts and costs. Lack of communication may prompt the party taking on the risk to overcharge in order to cover themselves against the unexpected, or factors that have not been clarified.

Insuring risks

Insuring risks is similar to transferring them, but rather than asking another company to take action if a risk occurs, you ask them to financially compensate you for its occurrence.

As with transferring, the company will want payment for taking on the risk in this way. This is a familiar concept from everyday life, where we have to insure our household goods, cars and mortgage repayments against a number of downside risks, from theft and accident to death.

Businesses also invest in many types of insurance, including public liability, employer's liability and so on.

Insurance is often a good response to operational risks. It is particularly appropriate for low-probability downsides with hugely significant impacts, such as a fire at the workplace.

Getting it right

Whatever approach you choose to the risks you face, there are central themes to risk management that have to be in place for it to be successful.

Effective decision making and risk management are based on understanding, information and consistency. It is vital that everyone involved is working from a shared idea of the significance of the risks facing the business, the probability of them occurring and the actions that they need to take in order to minimise downsides (or maximise upsides).

Below are some questions to ask in key areas to assess your risk management capabilities:

- [ ] **understanding operational risk:**

  - [ ] are the risks that can arise in key business processes understood?
  - [ ] are the implications of choosing or creating particular new processes understood?
  - [ ] are the impacts of operational risk understood, in terms of their immediate impact and also any potential impacts at higher levels?

- [ ] **understanding strategic risk:**

  - [ ] are decision makers aware of the strategic risks facing the business?
  - [ ] are the implications of 'doing nothing' or continuing along the present course understood?
  - [ ] has 'business as usual' been examined in the same way as a 'risky' new direction would be?
  - [ ] have the risks implied simply by entering or remaining in a particular market been examined?

- [ ] **understanding probability:**

  - [ ] have probabilities been quantified in a consistent way, that allows for comparison?
  - [ ] what evidence is there to support estimates of probability?
  - [ ] where there is uncertainty, has this been understood and acknowledged by decision makers?
  - [ ] is there shared understanding of the subjectivity involved in probability calculations?

- [ ] **understanding impact:**
  - [ ] have impacts been quantified wherever possible, to allow for comparison?
  - [ ] is it clear where risks might impact on more than one area of the business?
  - [ ] is there the potential for risks to have interdependencies, making the occurrence of two or more risks together more significant?
  - [ ] are the different levels of impact understood (operations, strategy, financial, cultural)?

- [ ] **information:**
  - [ ] **documenting:** how will risks, responses and results be documented? what procedures will be used for recording the actions taken to manage risks and their results?
  - [ ] **sharing:** how will information on risks and the success (or otherwise) of particular responses be disseminated throughout the business, to avoid duplication of effort?
  - [ ] **communicating:** who owns key information? who does it need to reach in order to support decisions on risk? what are the best media, formats and techniques for communicating?

- [ ] **clear roles and responsibilities:**
  - [ ] whose **responsibility** is each risk? who 'owns' it by default?
  - [ ] who has enough **authority** and/or information to take a decision on how risks will be managed?
  - [ ] **who will take action** to manage the risk? who will become its new 'owner'?

- [ ] **reporting and monitoring:**
  - [ ] who needs to know what, and when?
  - [ ] what is the best medium or channel to provide information on risks, such that those who need to take decisions have the information they need in a format they will find conducive?

- [ ] **consistency of approach:**
  - [ ] if similar risks occur in different parts of the business, is the response the same?
  - [ ] could risks easily be aggregated across the business if this kind of concentration brought benefits?

consistency of analysis:

- where possible, are risks assessed using standard, objective criteria, or at least those that are agreed by all within the business?

consistency of tools and techniques:

- where decision-making tools are used, are they used in a consistent way across departments and teams?
- is there a genuine shared perspective on risks that affect different groups?

consistency of terminology:

- are risks described in terms that allow meaningful comparison and evaluation across the business?
- are common terms used with the same sense throughout the business?
- are there any aspects that need to be quantified, or made less subjective, to allow for more focused discussion between those involved?

Read more :

The Art of Modeling with Spreadsheets

by Stephen G. Powell
and Kenneth R. Baker

Looking back:

Key ideas from this chapter

- There are several possible responses to risk, ranging from tolerating to eliminating.

- The right response to a risk depends on the specific situation and also our calculations of probability and impact.

- Transferring and insuring against risk involve others in risks, to the benefit of the business; the trade-off is increased costs.

- Managing risks well depends on sharing information, clear responsibilities and consistency of approach.

5 Risk psychology:

The last two chapters have focused on analysing risks and decisions with as much objectivity as possible. But the way we deal with risk is often far removed from this ideal. This chapter looks at how and why this happens, and what you can do about it.

The personal perspective

Risk and uncertainty are not encountered only in the business world – we deal with them every day in normal life, in situations where they have a much more direct, immediately felt impact than is usually the case in business. Areas of personal life where we deal with risk are:

- [ ] **recreational:** hobbies and activities; dangerous pursuits

- [ ] **financial:** savings; investments; property; pensions

- [ ] **health:** lifestyle choices (diet, exercise, smoking); decisions about medical care

- [ ] **safety:** in the home; when travelling

- [ ] **career:** moving between jobs; starting a new career; investing time or money in gaining new skills

- [ ] **social:** choice of friends or partner; family decisions; decisions affecting reputation and personal standing.

As a result of considering and responding to these types of risk in our lives, we build an intuitive understanding of concepts such as probability and impact, but it is normally fairly vague, and we are only half-conscious of our reasoning processes. As our memories accumulate, we also adopt beliefs, perceptions and attitudes that affect the decisions we take. Over time, we build up a 'natural' approach to making decisions that feels 'right' to us. But this approach isn't always useful when transferred across to the business realm; in fact, it can be disastrous. The rest of this chapter looks at why this is so, and what we can do about it.

Personal values

Values are beliefs that we hold that tell us what we should do in a range of situations.

Business decisions are governed as much by the values held by those within the business as by the facts. We don't become robots when we walk through the door at work. We want to feel that we have made an impact on the business, and that our contribution has been in tune with our beliefs. This puts values at the heart of every decision.

We form values early in life, and they tend not to change – they are one of the most constant elements of our personalities. One way that values can change is when they are in conflict with other aspects of ourselves; for example, our ideas of what we 'could' be (our dreams and ambitions) may push us away from what we 'should' do (our values).

When we are faced with a new type of decision, or a decision where information is limited, it is our values that guide us. We cannot choose between courses of action without criteria to evaluate the alternatives facing us, and values provide them. For example, if we value the environment, our choice of car might be dictated by its carbon monoxide emission levels – our values help us make a choice.

However, values go deeper than this. They also affect how we process information about the world – how we select, organise and use facts to make decisions. A decision may not be a simple case of applying our values to the facts – what facts we use, and how we use them, are also affected by our values.

We may choose a cleaner car because we value the environment, and we are likely to state this openly. But other values, perhaps including the work ethic that gets us to work on time or the family values that make us want to get home quickly, are in play too. They mean that other alternatives, such as cycling or walking to work, don't even get mentioned. It is these hidden values – the ones we don't talk about or aren't aware of – that can affect our decisions most profoundly. The other sections in this chapter explore this theme more fully.

Corporate values

Just as individuals have values, so do businesses. These often reflect the values of the founder or leader of the business. As a business adds more people to its operation, it naturally tends to choose those with similar values. Conversely, those with dissimilar values are either not selected to join, or don't stay long when they do. Over time, this results in the organisation having a recognisable set of values. Individuals with values that are at odds with those of the organisation will often find it difficult to fit in or make progress.

Corporate values affect decisions at all levels and can have a profound impact on the progress and fortunes of the business. They find expression in the choices that are made in key areas, including:

- [ ] **new directions:** chosen areas for expansion and consolidation; unfavoured areas of business activity

- [ ] **recognition and reward:** the attitudes, behaviours and achievements that are most encouraged and rewarded

- [ ] **risk aversion or appetite:** attitudes to risk exposure and the possibility of loss; attitudes to those who make mistakes

- [ ] **leadership:** the personalities of those who become leaders within the business

- [ ] **altruism:** activities carried out for the good of the community in which the business operates, rather than its own direct benefit; policies on sustainability and the environment

- [ ] **diversity:** in the workforce as a whole; among management

- [ ] **relationships:** the nature and tone of relationships with customers, suppliers, partners and competitors.

Often, the meanings ascribed to commonly used terms can help to reveal corporate values. What do terms such as 'quality', 'good practice', 'value', 'improvement', 'risk' and 'success' actually mean in your business?

Business cultures that successfully reproduce their values among their people are in a good position to respond to changes in the business environment, since every decision maker is in tune with the values of the organisation and can make informed choices in whatever situation they face. At their strongest, shared values can even offer a viable alternative to 'command and control' modes of management.

Conversely, values that fail to 'take root' in the organisation, or that become empty statements that are visibly disconnected with the reality 'on the ground', are less helpful. Also, out-of-date values can become rigid dogmas that just tie people down rather than helping them make decisions.

Frames

Frames are the limits and filters we put around reality to simplify it and help us move towards a decision in complex circumstances. They enable us to make decisions, while at the same time limiting us to a particular perspective. Frames dictate the alternatives that we give ourselves, and those we don't; this in turn affects the information we seek out when making a decision and the choice that we eventually make.

We briefly encountered the effects of framing in chapter 3, with the decision tree relating to a company moving to new premises. As we saw, the tree only looked at a limited number of alternatives; it simplified the decision hugely. There were probably other premises available, and what about the alternatives for outsourcing, looking at alternative business processes or optimising existing ones, changing the skill-sets of those working in the company and so on? These choices were excluded from the frame in order to focus attention on the key issues of the decision.

There could also be completely different ways of framing that decision. We examined it in terms of increasing profit within a particular timescale, but any other measure of success, within any other boundary (temporal or otherwise), might have served. Others, such as employees, might look at the impacts of the decision in completely different terms – personal convenience or upheaval, for example. Frames foreground particular aspects of a decision and hide others.

In business, this kind of framing can have a huge impact. It's one thing to make the right decisions when faced with a number of alternatives, but what if the direction you should be taking hasn't even been identified as a possibility? For businesses setting their strategic direction for the future, this is crucial; they need to frame their decisions in such a way that allows the right alternative to be uncovered. But frames can often be hard to perceive; it can be difficult to tell when we are limiting our own perceptions.

Frames also have implications for building commitment to decisions. Frames aren't always universally shared; people will favour alternatives that fit into their own perspectives. When we say we 'don't see eye to eye' with people, or that we are 'talking at cross purposes', this often means we don't share the same frames. Differing frames are at the heart of many personal disagreements.

Frames can't be avoided, but they can be worked with. The first step is to uncover them; they can be found in:

- **assumptions** that people hold, whether made explicit or not

- the **yardsticks and benchmarks** used to assess performance and achievement

- **priorities** and **pet projects**

- **unwritten rules**; things that are 'off the radar'

- **prevalent ways of thinking**, such as industry norms, accepted codes of behaviour, independent standards and so on.

In any decision situation, you need to try and ensure that you are using the right frame, and change to a different frame if necessary. The 'right' frame is one that fits the problem at hand, allowing you to bring in all the relevant information in a balanced way and reach the right conclusion. Communication is key here; sharing perceptions helps to bring frames to the fore and establish when they are not going to be useful in decision making.

Read more :
Winning Decisions
by J. Edward Russo and Paul J.H. Schoemaker

Prospect theory

Prospect theory relates to whether we frame the outcomes of our decisions in terms of potential loss (threat) or potential gain (opportunity). Although this may seem to be a simple equivalent form of words, behavioural researchers Daniel Kahneman and Amos Tversky found that in fact it can have a powerful effect on how people make decisions. We do not evaluate gains and losses as equal in value, like pluses and minuses on a balance sheet. Experiments show that we hate to lose more than we love to win.

Prospect theory states that people value a gain that is certain (i.e. one that doesn't involve any risk) more than a gain that is uncertain, even though the uncertain gain has a larger expected value. But for losses, the reverse is true: people prefer an uncertain loss to a certain loss, even when the uncertain loss could potentially be more damaging than the certain one.

Framing a situation in terms of loss, as opposed to gain, powerfully affects behaviour. A study showed that significantly more people will pay for loft insulation if failing to do so is framed as losing them money, rather than insulating the loft as gaining extra cash.

Managers have been shown to pay far more attention to potential losses than potential gains, as is well known on the trading floors of finance houses where traders have to be taught to go against risk instincts. Instinct is inclined to chase losses and take profits too early, so traders have to be forcefully encouraged to take risks: 'cut your losses and let your profits run'.

So our decisions can depend on whether we view alternative outcomes as losses or gains. In business terms, it is easy to see how particular decisions might be framed in different ways:

- [ ] **growing the business:** threat of losing investment, or opportunity to realise more profit?

- [ ] **not growing the business:** threat of stagnation and decline, or opportunity to consolidate and build core strengths?

- [ ] **appointing young managers:** threat of bad decisions being made, or opportunity to harness innovation?

- [ ] **retaining older managers:** threat of failing to innovate, or opportunity to harness experience and learning?

The lesson is to think carefully about how decisions are framed, and perhaps consider framing them in more than one way to try and identify the effects that prospect theory has on the alternatives that people prefer.

Read more :

Choices, Values and Frames

edited by Daniel Kahneman and Amos Tversky

Risk aversion

Risk aversion means avoiding risks because of the fear of loss, or equating risk taking with loss. Risk-averse decision makers tend to avoid taking risks, even when the expected value of taking the risk and the certain value of avoiding it are equal – or, in some circumstances, avoiding risk when it would be better to take it.

Let's return once more to dice game version A from chapter 3. It has a positive expected value (0.66). If you play it 100 times, you will probably be around £66 'up' – give or take a few pounds. Now, given the choice between playing 100 times and being given £66, the risk-averse decision maker opts for the certain £66 rather than run the risk

of winning less. But those with a stronger risk appetite, or risk preference, opt to play the game in the hope of winning more. Risk-neutral individuals, realising that the expected value of both the game and the £66 gift are objectively equal, have no preference.

Risk aversion has its roots in our past. Like all animal species, and especially those engaged in competition for scarce resources, we are more sensitive to the danger of loss than the possibility of gain. In many environments and contexts, losses are irrecoverable, which may be life-threatening under subsistence conditions. This deep-seated aversion to loss feeds through into our risk decisions.

In business decision making, risk aversion can be manifested wherever there is subjectivity or uncertainty. The aversion to risk leads us to create or favour estimates, analyses or conclusions that discourage taking risks:

☐ overestimating the probability or impact of negative outcomes; underestimating the probability or impact of positive outcomes

☐ failing to compare the expected value of a risk and the value of not taking it, or distorting such a comparison when it is made

- denigrating or casting doubt on information that suggests risk taking is worth while; seeking, promoting and amplifying information that discourages risk taking

- dwelling on past risks that resulted in downsides; 'forgetting' past risks that resulted in upsides

- assigning greater weight to recent negative outcomes of risk taking (however insignificant) than past upside outcomes (however significant).

Risk aversion threatens the rationality of decision making. At its worst, it turns the decision-making process into a battle between the heart and the head, with the heart counselling caution even though the head realises a risk is worth taking. Although we may know from our analysis that a risk has a positive expected value, making it worth taking, we may find ourselves focusing on the potential downside to such an extent that we find it difficult to accept the risk.

Risk aversion is the driving force behind the insurance industry. We are often willing to pay insurance premiums that outweigh the expected value of the risks they are aimed at managing. In other words, based on objective probabilities and impacts, we are better off accepting many everyday risks than paying what we do to minimise their impacts should they occur. We are willing (eager, in fact) to do this because the potential losses (theft, fire, illness, death) are so emotive that they drive out any analytical thoughts of probability and impact – if we have them at all.

The problem with information

It seems obvious to say that having more information about a situation helps you make a better decision. It has been a recurrent theme in this book. But 'getting information' is not as neutral a process as the phrase makes it sound. The ways in which we select and present information, make comparisons, assess relative value and (having done so) make risk decisions are often highly irrational.

We need information to make decisions, but we also need to know the limits of the information we have available, and the limits of our own objectivity. Armed with this understanding, we have to try to fill in the gaps and fight against our own in-built biases.

In fact, an understanding of what we do and don't know can sometimes be more important than the amount of data at our disposal – intelligence is more useful than information.

Confirmation bias

As we have seen in this book, uncertainty is everywhere and unceasing. Information bombards us; we have to filter it in order to feel some faith in the rightness of our decisions. Once we've settled on a particular course of action, every piece of information we find out that confirms it is pleasing to us; it makes us feel that our decision is the right one. So we seek out, or favour, such information. Conversely, every piece of information that disconfirms it is unwelcome and discomfiting; it throws us back into doubt and indecision. As a result, such information (negative feedback, for example) is neglected, ignored or denigrated.

Research shows that many decisions are taken incredibly quickly. Information gained 'to help us decide' is actually being gathered to back up a decision that has already been taken. An example of this is interview situations, where a decision on an applicant is often made very early in the meeting, and subsequent questions are aimed at backing up this decision, or reassuring the interviewer, rather than challenging it.

In other situations, gathering information is done in order to demonstrate that decisions are being taken rigorously, even though they have already been taken. The decision maker who wishes to appear rigorous will not state their position until 'enough' information has been gathered to 'confirm' it; they may not even admit to themselves that they have decided until an appropriate amount of information has been obtained.

Anchors

Anchors are the starting points for assessments of value, gain and loss. An example from everyday life is the estate agent's valuation of a house, which establishes the starting point for discussions of the sale price. Unfortunately, we tend to seize on any available information with which to anchor our considerations, regardless of its accuracy or even its relevance to the issue at hand. For example, a study asked people to guess how many

African nations were part of the UN, but first they were asked whether their guess was higher or lower than a randomly generated number. Their guesses were 'pulled' towards the random number, which acted as an anchor despite its complete irrelevance.

Poorly chosen anchors lead us into problems with framing and prospect effects, as we try to evaluate potential 'gains' and 'losses' from a starting point that is arbitrary or inaccurate.

Certain types of information are particularly likely to act as anchors:

- [ ] the **first information** that becomes available when we start thinking about a decision

- [ ] the **most readily available** information ('availability bias')

- [ ] the **most recently obtained** information (the 'recency effect')

- [ ] **vivid** information such as that heard from a trusted friend, delivered face-to-face or carrying some kind of emotional force.

Even when we realise that we have fallen prey to anchoring, we still have a problem. We know we need to adjust our thinking 'away' from the anchor, but by doing so we are still basing our thinking around it. Ideally we would be able to forget it through effort of will, but this is impossible; the next best thing is to find more information that suggests other anchors, to achieve some sort of balance.

Over-reacting to bad news

Recently obtained or particularly vivid information can anchor decisions. Because of prospect theory and/or risk aversion, this effect is sharpened when such information is negative – when we hear bad news. Because of our deep-seated fear of loss, we react quickly and excessively to bad news, and slowly to good news. This is a familiar phenomenon in stock markets, where prices often tumble in reaction to poor earnings reports.

We instinctively seek order and patterns in what happens to us, so our over-reaction to bad news often makes us think that a new pattern is emerging in events: that the 'tide is turning' or that 'things are changing'. In fact we are often just witnessing a chance occurrence; such events leap to our attention because they are unusual or exceptional, and we make them more significant than they are.

Real life : The risk psychology of a rogue trader

The spectacular collapse of Barings Bank in February 1995 showed what can happen when companies fail to manage risk. The enormous losses run up by a single trader remained unsuspected for an astonishingly long time; finally, the world-famous bank collapsed, with debts in excess of £800 million.

Barings, the world's first merchant bank, was founded in 1763. With clients including governments and royalty, it became the epitome of tradition and stability. Nick Leeson joined the company in 1989, aged 22. After a spell in Jakarta, he made his mark in London as a settlements expert in futures and options. In 1992 he was offered the job of setting up and managing an operation in Singapore, where he built up a reputation in fast-growing markets. Leeson was tasked not only with leading the trading team, but also with settlements: a dual role that involved a substantial concentration of powers and the scope to evade controls. In July 1994, an internal audit report flagged up the risk of this, but the warning went unheeded. By that time, Nick Leeson had already run up and concealed losses in excess of £50 million.

Almost as soon as he arrived in Singapore, Leeson started taking unauthorised speculative positions, covering up losses while reporting impressive profits. He later claimed that he was motivated by the desire to cover up errors and make good his losses. However, in mid-1993 he managed to turn losses of £6 million into a profit – but continued to speculate. Losses crept up again, reaching £23 million by February 1994 and £200 million by early 1995. Leeson dealt in unhedged positions and doubled the stakes following a loss. Losses spiralled to £600 million.

In January 1995 concerns were voiced by the Singapore International Monetary Exchange and auditors Coopers & Lybrand. Finally, an earthquake in Kobe saw the market tumble. Leeson fabricated correspondence in an attempt to cover his tracks from Coopers, and on Thursday 23 February fled to Malaysia with his wife. He was jailed in Singapore in 1999.

Nick Leeson exhibited many problems associated with bad decision making:

- [ ] **overconfidence:** as a result of his early successes, Leeson was supremely confident of his abilities; he later boasted, 'I was probably the only person... able to operate on both sides of the balance sheet'

- [ ] **overestimating probabilities:** Leeson consistently overestimated the likelihood of making a profit

- [ ] **underestimating impact:** he seemed to be unaware of the magnitude of what he was doing

- [ ] **inappropriate responses to risk:** Leeson's failure to hedge against his risks left him exposed

- [ ] **escalation of commitment:** Leeson ploughed on in the belief that his losses would 'come good'; his faith in his own abilities (coupled with some disdain for his managers) made this a point of pride

- [ ] **deviance:** Leeson was of a character to bend rules to his own advantage.

Compounding all these problems were Leeson's own values. Unregulated by his superiors, he failed to set his own boundaries and slipped from bad risk management into criminality.

Leeson's managers also exhibited problems of their own:

- [ ] **selective use of information:** they were unwilling to look behind the mask of his success

- [ ] **ill-advised or tacit risk transfer:** they did not have enough business knowledge to understand the risks Leeson was taking

- [ ] **overconfidence and complacency:** Barings' long history may have made managers feel invulnerable

- [ ] **inconsistency of approach:** hazy reporting lines and a lack of supervision were compounded by an inconsistent matrix management structure; different cultures and processes existed in different parts of the organisation.

The Barings story also illustrates vividly why good processes for risk management are vital. The problems should have been picked up at the operational level, but instead grew until they became a strategic risk.

Read more :

All that glitters: The fall of Barings

by John Gapper and Nicholas Denton

Affection for the status quo

In many situations, we will strongly favour the situation we are in over the opportunity to change. In this frame of mind, we tend to emphasise the danger of change, or the proven benefits of the status quo. Even when change is objectively more likely to bring us benefit, we will often stick with the status quo 'to see how things work out', deferring, avoiding or denying the choices that we have. We may also fall prey to confirmation bias, seeking information that supports the status quo and ignoring the reasons to change.

It seems strange in a society that so values and eulogises choice, but there is a sense in which people don't like to make decisions. Our brains are not built for mathematical weighing of alternatives; we like our choices simple, so we can evaluate which alternatives are better or worse for us quickly. Simple either/or decisions (should we develop this new product or not?) are less daunting than multi-alternative decisions (which new product should we develop?). Research shows that the more alternatives are available to people, the more likely they are to do nothing. Faced with a huge range of alternatives, we often simply cling to what we know.

The other reason for liking the status quo is regret aversion, or the fear of making a wrong choice. We are mindful of the possibility of future regret at negative outcomes resulting from our own choices. Unnecessary insurance and product guarantees are sold on this basis.

The endowment effect

The endowment effect is the tendency to overvalue what we own. Consider a possession of yours that has value – a car, perhaps. What is it worth, in your opinion? Now imagine that someone is offering you a similar car for sale – same model, same age, same wear and tear. What would you pay for it?

Similar to affection for the status quo, the endowment effect leads us to try and hang on to what we have, even when something else might be better. As with other biases, we are likely to seek information that supports this emotion. We will probably also demand inflated returns, or bigger positive impacts, from new, 'risky' alternatives, to offset the sense of sacrifice we feel when letting go of what is ours.

The hazard of this bias is opportunity cost – chances to make improvements or turn a profit go begging, while you doggedly hang on to what you already have.

Bigness bias

This strange term refers to the inconsistency with which we evaluate objectively equal values when they are set 'beside' larger values. There are many ready examples from everyday life. While we may carefully check restaurant bills to make sure they are accurate to the penny, we may increase the value of bids we make for houses by thousands of pounds at a time, and with less thought.

The size of the overall amount involved sets the standard by which we evaluate the significance of changes, rather than their objective value. (The amount may not be financial; the problem can occur with anything that is quantified.) Bigness bias in business can see us ignore or fail to investigate fees added on to high-value contracts, for example, before moving on to obsess over the price we pay for stationery. The amounts involved may be comparable, and the potential impact on the business therefore also the same, but context dictates how seriously we take these objectively similar amounts.

Mental accounting

Mental accounting concerns the way we regard money (and perhaps other resources) differently depending on its origins and history. It is related to anchoring: we regard gains or profits (assessed relative to an anchor) as being somehow less important or significant than 'real' money; as a result we are more likely to take big risks with them.

For example, consider the scenario of finding money behind a sofa cushion. We feel a strange delight, as if we have been given a gift, even though we are re-finding our own lost money, that we earned with the same effort as all our other money. Because it is a 'free gift', we are more likely to treat it more frivolously – by spending it on a night out, perhaps – than the same amount sitting in our savings account. We exhibit similar biases in other situations, for example regarding an inheritance as a cue to take on volatile investments that we would never consider putting our 'hard-earned' cash into.

Mental accounting puts the concept of personal values and risk appetite, which we looked at earlier in this chapter, in a new light. We do have preferences about the risks we will accept or seek out, but they change with our emotions and in response to events.

Overconfidence

We need to have confidence in order to take decisions. If we cannot remove the subjectivity from a situation, or getting all the information would take too long, our values and self-confidence are the only way to build a bridge from indecision to action. We need to have faith in our own ability to make decisions – otherwise uncertainty would paralyse us, condemning us to a perpetual state of indecision and interia. And indeed, if you ask a decision maker whether they are good at making decisions, they will generally say yes – that belief is the reason they wanted to make decisions in the first place.

Unfortunately, we are prone to overconfidence in our abilities. The advice in this book to seek information and weigh decisions with objectivity is designed to counter that very problem. But wherever there is subjectivity, overconfidence can distort a decision. It takes the form of overestimating the probability and impact of upsides (or

underestimating downsides). Information is marshalled to support the overconfident position, to make it seem reasonable.

A problem with overconfidence is that it becomes stronger when we face issues of moderate or extreme difficulty or unfamiliarity – in other words, the less competent we are to deal with a situation, the more likely we are to believe (wrongly) that we can. But when we are on familiar ground, or dealing with problems that we know about, we are less likely to be overconfident.

If you suspect that you yourself may be overconfident, ask a colleague who you respect to play 'devil's advocate' and argue against your position. This should be done on the understanding that the aim is to find the best way forward, not win the argument or 'score points'.

Read more :

Judgment in Managerial Decision Making

by Max H. Bazerman

Illusions of control

The illusion of control is a particularly dangerous form of overconfidence: the tendency to act as though chance events can be personally controlled. It arises as a result of making arbitrary and unfounded causal links between particular outcomes to particular actions in the past – the foundation of many superstitions.

As with many of the other psychological problems described in this chapter, this bias has its roots in our evolutionary development. To survive in a hostile environment, we needed to make decisions quickly and also feel secure in the choices that we made. The more control we have (or think we have), the more faith we have in our own decisions. We want to feel good about our decision-making ability, so we pretend that we have more control than we really do.

The illusion of control is most dangerous when we are dealing with situations that we objectively have no way of controlling (rather than those where we could, theoretically, affect the outcome). Examples of uncontrollable situations would include the roll of a dice (or any other game of pure chance), the weather and the stock market. Faced with such situations, our instinct is to try and control them, or 'discover' patterns in them when there are none. Plus, we are predisposed to believe that this is possible.

If a decision maker develops illusions of control, they begin to believe that they can predict unpredictable events, such as the roll of a dice, with more accuracy than is actually possible. Sometimes, gathering and analysing information (a good idea in theory) contributes to this sense of heightened personal power or prescience.

Some people are more prone to this problem than others, but there are also external factors that can lead to it:

☐ **stress:** stressful situations are those where we have too much work and not enough control over it; by convincing us that even our most hasty, ill-considered decisions are right, the illusion of control restores the balance between workload and ability

☐ **competition:** competitive situations suggest to us that control is possible, and that being a 'winner' or a 'loser' is a matter of personal ability or effort (the 'competitor' may not be human, for example gamblers aiming to 'beat' a casino through some kind of system)

- **focusing on outcomes:** if the short-term results of decisions are rewarded (rather than the quality of decision making), people are discouraged from seeking more information about a decision; instead they develop the illusion that positive outcomes are the results of their own abilities, and that they don't need to think deeply about decisions

- **choice, involvement and familiarity:** the illusion of control is stronger when we have more choices to make, more involvement in the situation, and more familiarity with the factors involved.

It follows from these points that some good ways to guard against the illusion of control include managing levels of stress in the workplace, discouraging personal competition and encouraging (perhaps rewarding) a considered, analytical approach to decisions.

Escalation of commitment

Problems can arise when people make a link between a direction that they favour and their own values, personality or reputation.
Once people make such a link, they find it difficult to step away from the choice they have made, since doing so would constitute weakness or defeat in their eyes.

Sometimes, a person caught in this situation will invest more and more commitment in their position, regardless of its merits, rather than backing down. Psychologists call this 'non-rational escalation of commitment'.

If you suspect that this might be going on, consider questions such as:

- what personal values might make this person favour certain alternatives?

- what past decisions or experiences might make them favour certain alternatives? what past mistakes might they be seeking to redress or cancel out? what do they have at stake (reputation, career, investment)?

- how can they show that their preferred alternative benefits the business as well as themselves? can they demonstrate a positive expected value?

- what are their attitudes to information that doesn't support their alternative (impatience, deliberate ignorance, denial)?

Identifying or restating the common interests (i.e. business benefit) that everyone shares can be helpful. Getting back in touch with any core values of the business may also help to put decisions back in context.

Faulty hindsight

As we've seen, the past is the only guide we have as to how the future will turn out. When faced with a new situation, we interpret it in terms of what has happened to us before; our values provide the bridge between what we know and the actions we need to take. But our memories aren't just data banks – we don't remember everything, and what we do recall isn't remembered objectively. We edit out or modify what we don't like and focus on those events that support what we want to do.

Just ask two people who have argued to tell you what happened. It's very likely that you will hear two very different accounts. As time goes by, stories change with the telling and perceptions are likely to drift even further apart.

The way we regard the past can influence decision making profoundly, but often we're not even aware of this. For our decisions to be balanced, we need to get to grips with the way past actions affect present decisions.

We can fall into several traps relating to our own place in the past. They all involve remembering past decisions or their consequences inaccurately, or selectively, with the benefit of hindsight. As time goes by, we can find ourselves slipping into traps including:

- [ ] **attribution error:** decisions that had bad outcomes were taken by others, not by us; they should take all the blame; the causes of problems are simple and personal rather than complex and environmental

- [ ] **hindsight bias:** decisions that had positive outcomes were taken by us; we foresaw negative outcomes at the time of the decisions that led to them ('I knew it all along!'); we had information at the time of the decision that has actually come to light since it was taken.

Sometimes these are deliberate distortions, sometimes they are subconscious self-protective behaviours, and sometimes they are genuine mistakes. They become stronger over time: past events become more distant and hazy, while perceptions strengthen as we mull over the past or discuss it with sympathetic colleagues.

To restore a balanced view of the past, consider these tactics:

- [ ] challenge and examine the **evidence of cause and effect**: did particular decisions really lead to current situations? what is the evidence for this?

- [ ] seek the **views of as many people as possible**, particularly those with experience that stretches back a long time in relevant areas; focus on areas of disagreement to uncover frames

- [ ] try to **shift the focus away from individuals** and their achievements or mistakes; reward good decision making rather than positive outcomes (see the next chapter)

- [ ] **document decision-making processes** to establish an objective record of what decisions were taken, who was involved and why.

Sunk costs

One key to understanding how the past affects the present is the concept of 'sunk costs'. This refers to the tendency to allow past investments or expenditure to affect decisions in the present. Even though every decision has to be taken on the basis of the factors present in the situation right now, the pull of past events can be very strong.

We need, wherever possible, to see decisions in terms of future benefit rather than past losses or gains. But we are often more likely to choose alternatives that are in line with our past spending rather than changing direction, because we don't like the idea that past investment is 'wasted', and wish to redeem it. This can lead us into the trap of 'throwing good money after bad', or 'honouring' sunk costs.

What has been invested need not be financial, or even tangible. In fact, we may feel a far stronger 'pull' from emotional investments than financial ones. For example, we might wish to continue with a project because of the time we have put into it and the attention we have lavished upon it, even though it has become clear that the probability of success is far lower than we had thought. The problem is that we have 'put something of ourselves into it'; to give up on it now is to give up on a part of ourselves. Obviously, these feelings are a long way from objective decision making.

Overcompensation (risk homeostasis)

It is widely believed that seat belts save lives. They do in their capacity to protect against crash injuries, but psychologists have shown that there is a disturbing other side to the data. It seems that seat belts, and other features that make cars feel like safe environments, induce increased risk taking driving behaviour, usually unconsciously. This is called 'risk homeostasis', a kind of dangerous overcompensation for risk protection.

Research backs this idea up; it has proved very difficult to establish for sure that seat belts really do save lives, however much we might feel instinctively that it 'must' be so. Many studies pointing towards a reduction in road deaths as a result of seat belts being introduced have subsequently been challenged. There are even some studies that show fatalities actually increasing when seat belt use increases, or is enforced.

The problem here is overcompensation: when we feel that one risk has been successfully managed, we sometimes feel justified in taking another risk, without considering that the expected value of the second decision cancels out the positive effect of the first. The overall effect is to increase our exposure to risk rather than decrease it.

This throws up interesting questions when we are trying to find responses to risk, particularly when we are considering 'hedging' one risk against another. We have to take the psychological sense of 'protection' that comes from taking action against risk into account, and aim to discern whether we are exposing ourselves to more risk without justification.

A more frivolous example from everyday life is the indulgent night out that follows a session at the gym. Believing ourselves somehow 'insured', we take a health risk that probably outweighs the positive impacts of our earlier actions.

The problems of risk homeostasis also highlight how our intuitions or instincts can betray us. We are most likely to fall into the trap of using information selectively when the conclusion to be drawn from it is 'obvious' to us – we simply edit out the information that does not support our view. When the conclusion to be drawn is deeply counter-intuitive we may simply refuse to accept it, even when hard evidence points to it.

The problem may be intensified when, as with the seat-belt issue, the conclusion is that actions we have taken with the intention of minimising probability or impact have actually had the opposite effect.

This can be a hazard when we are trying to decide whether to change long-established approaches or business processes in business. It becomes so 'evident' or 'obvious' to us that they are as good as they can be, and that actions to change them could not result in any improvement, that we simply don't consider information suggesting otherwise. Or, if we are taking action to change, we may be unwilling to accept that our actions aren't having the desired consequences.

Read more:
Risk
by John Adams

Restoring the balance

This chapter has focused on the psychological traps that afflict decision makers. What can we do to avoid them? All the answers focus on balance: getting more information, different types of information, and more people involved in decisions in order to redress the biases to which individuals are often prone:

- ☐ bringing as much **information on probabilities and impacts** to the decision-making process as possible; using recognised third-party authorities where possible to emphasise objectivity

- ☐ ensuring that the **upside** of risks receives the same coverage as the **downside**

- ☐ using **statistics** and techniques such as the decision tree to structure decisions clearly

- ☐ asking '**disconfirming questions**': try to undermine the basis for the chosen alternative, and see how it holds up under pressure

- ☐ actively seeking out **information that supports other alternatives**

- ☐ trying out **different theories and hypotheses** to see what other outcomes the available information supports, or what information you might be missing

- ☐ gathering a **balanced selection of information** on the benefits (positive impacts) and downsides (negative impacts) of all possible outcomes (insofar as is practical and affordable)

- [ ] using **information systems that encourage completeness and balance** rather than allowing incompleteness; ensuring that data used to support decisions is representative

- [ ] **sharing knowledge about decision making:** examining other people's knowledge and its limits, and encouraging them to do the same for you; sharing knowledge about prospect theory, anchoring, overconfidence and so on

- [ ] applying the same **procedures** to recording, analysing and considering all the information relating to a decision – supporting or otherwise

- [ ] remaining open to **new information**

- [ ] appealing to **reason;** encouraging everyone to aim for objectivity about risks and decisions; using tools to increase objectivity

- [ ] **challenging assumptions,** or predictions of future scenarios based on past events

- [ ] asking for **evidence** to back up impressions and perceptions.

Looking back:

Key ideas from this chapter

- [ ] The responses we have developed to risk in everyday life may not help us make business decisions well.

- [ ] Our personal values, and those of the organisations we work in, have a profound impact on our decisions.

- [ ] The way we frame decisions dictates the alternatives we can consider and the way we consider them.

- [ ] We don't always process information well when making decisions; this problem needs to be managed.

6 When things go wrong:

Every cloud has a silver lining, because every mistake is an opportunity to learn. This chapter looks at how good risk management and informed decision making can help you learn from errors.

Human errors

Management and behavioural thinker Michael Frese's work has focused on errors and their management. He defines an error as an unintentional deviation from a goal, caused by an act or omission that is in principle avoidable.

Errors happen when we make decisions. By improving the way we make decisions, we can try to prevent errors, or minimise their probability. By improving the way we respond when things go wrong, we can try to manage errors, or minimise their impact. We can also try to create positive impacts in negative situations, by taking the opportunities for learning that mistakes provide.

As we have seen in this book, preventing errors by good decision making is not easy. Our brains aren't computers; they are poor at calculating probabilities, thinking of different possible outcomes and holding lots of information. Situations that are complex, or constantly changing, confuse us even further.

Throughout this book we've seen how our 'natural' decision-making processes are often false friends in business. To help our brains get to grips with uncertainty, we have to create mathematical and logical structures. The fact that these are hard to understand indicates how 'unnatural' they are for us. Our brains are designed for self-preservation – taking decisions quickly, under pressure – to ensure survival. To do this, we take 'cognitive shortcuts' that allow us to cut through the information we're facing and reach a decision. The problem is that we often make the wrong choice; we looked at some reasons for this in the last chapter.

It's the same story with error prevention. When things go wrong, many 'natural' responses, such as blaming others, are self-preservation impulses. They won't help us to learn from our mistakes or share learning with others. To do so, we have to overcome our 'natural' responses and adopt approaches that can, at first sight, seem counter-intuitive.

Read more :

The Blackwell Dictionary of Organisational Behaviour (2nd edition)

edited by Nigel Nicholson, Pino Audia and Madan Pillutla

No blame

Errors arise when individuals make decisions, but their root causes are deeper than how 'competent' we are at the point when we make decisions. Their sources include many of the topics we've covered in this book:

- the **tools** available to help us make decisions (such as the decision tree)

- the **information** we have at our disposal

- our **psychological make-up:** our values; the way we use information; the frames we deploy; our memories and how we regard past events

- the **organisational context:** corporate values; support systems; the way decisions and their results are analysed and rewarded.

When things go wrong attribution makes us simplify all this hugely, by seeking the causes of negative outcomes in other people. There is always pressure to demonstrate a response to downsides, and people often find it hard not to blame those who took decisions perceived as having led to them. Our brains like simple causal stories, not ambiguous complexity, and it doesn't get much simpler than attributing downsides to the actions of someone else. The implication is that the error has arisen because an individual is deficient in character or ability ('look what you've done!').

Because being blamed gives rise to negative emotions, and often leads to some kind of sanction or punishment as well, people who make errors tend to blame them on circumstances or events, rather than themselves ('it's not my fault!').

Neither of these all-too-familiar 'natural' perspectives on error is useful in improving the way we make decisions, or the way we respond when things go wrong. Refraining from blame is a crucial part of informed decision making and good management.

Blame is counterproductive and damaging for several reasons:

- [ ] it has a **negative emotional impact** on the person concerned, making them more likely to 'self-regulate' their future behaviour in a limiting way

- [ ] it **closes down the discussions** that should result from mistakes

- [ ] it shifts the spotlight away from **analysis, learning and objectivity**

- [ ] it **discourages other people** in the business from taking any kind of risk, whatever the expected value.

If decisions are based on careful, objective consideration of probabilities and impacts, and the potential downside of a risk is accepted because of its positive overall value, then there should be no blame if this downside actually comes about.

Decision tools such as the decision tree create joint commitment to an action, so that no one person's position or reputation is on the line if things go wrong. In effect, this approach transfers business risks from the individual decision maker, who has much to lose from downsides occurring, to the business as a whole, which can absorb the impacts of downsides (both financial and reputational).

Good risk management is about being prepared for problems, which in turn helps to avoid a culture of blame. By valuing control, analysis and objectivity, the focus can be kept on the problems that everyone in the business faces together.

Some themes of a no-blame culture include:

- discussion of risks (and responsibilities for them) **before** problems arise, rather than afterwards

- emphasising **collective responsibility** and shared business goals

- aiming for **insights and understanding** about decisions, arrived at through a process of **co-operation and collaboration**

- acceptance of a **joint commitment** for taking specific actions, with no-one putting their 'head on the block' (regardless of any individual responsibilities that are assigned)

- **using tools** (such as the decision tree) to generate and confirm a joint commitment to decisions

- taking risks in an **informed** way, with full knowledge of the potential consequences

- when problems arise from particular decisions, **remembering and re-stating the reasoning** that went into those decisions

- aiming to draw **collective learning** rather than individual advantage from mistakes, problems and negative situations

- using **passive language** to defuse tensions and sidestep the assignation of blame (e.g. 'there is a problem' rather than 'so-and-so has made a mistake')

- understanding that **creativity, innovation and new directions** imply some freedom to make mistakes

- thinking of ways to **reward people on the basis of how well they take decisions,** not the results of those decisions.

Towards better decision making

In business, we tend to judge people by the results of their actions. Many performance management systems are oriented in this way, placing a strong emphasis on management by results. Realise upsides and you reap rewards and promotion; realise downsides and you are blamed and maybe even fired.

To most managers, this seems a natural way to 'encourage' and 'motivate' people to 'improve'.

If we reframe the argument in terms of decision quality, rather than result quality, the picture changes. People's 'mistakes' indicate that they are willing to make decisions, and it is only by making decisions and observing the results that we can improve. We learn about novel, unfamiliar or complex things through experiment and error.

As a London Business School study of financial traders showed, it is a serious error for decision makers to assume that bad results mean a bad strategy, just as it is to assume that making money was because you have a good strategy. In business, as in markets, luck plays a part, and the best managers are like the best traders in having an accurate and sufficiently modest view of which results to attribute to skill, and which to serendipity.

Business results are the outcome of the interaction between our decisions, our actions and chance. Even if we make no error, there is always the chance that a bad outcome will result from a 'good' decision. For example, we might play dice game version A from chapter 3 ten times and lose every time, despite having established that the risk had a positive expected value. But how would such a decision be regarded in business?

If we were rewarded solely on results, with no attention paid to the way we took our decisions, our £10 loss would look pretty bad. Our performance report might read as follows: 'Despite your poor results, you played this game again and again, throwing good money after bad on the off-chance of things somehow coming right. You recklessly gambled company money on an uncertain future. Your poor results are evidence of your bad judgement. What were you thinking?'

But if we were rewarded on the quality of our decision-making process, our actions would appear in a very different light, resulting in a different review: 'Although results have been poor, due to circumstances beyond your control, the quality of your decision making was excellent. You obtained all the information that you could on possible outcomes, and the probabilities of each, and took a decision on that basis. The negative results, though disappointing, have not bankrupted the company. You will be rewarded on the basis of decision-making quality.'

The flip side of this is that people might make decisions on impulse, or randomly, and still get good results by chance. By rewarding or promoting these individuals, the business risks having lucky managers rather than competent ones – fine, until their luck runs out. Also, although spontaneous decisions may turn out to bring some business benefit, they don't teach us anything. We can't use them to improve the way we take decisions, or to instruct others.

The implications for businesses are profound. If it is the quality of decision making, rather than results, that are the measure of success, then those who take decisions in the right way should be rewarded, even if they make mistakes. They should also be given more decisions to make in the future, not fewer.

This doesn't mean automatically promoting people who get bad results. It means:

- [ ] **encouraging better decision making** and making it clear that it will be rewarded

- [ ] setting **boundaries** to limit the impact that mistakes can have; acknowledging and actively **managing the risk** of mistakes

- [ ] avoiding or limiting exposure to **fatal downsides** (doctors and airline pilots, for example, need systems to help them avoid errors)

- [ ] when rewarding people, considering the **way decisions have been taken** as well as the results of decisions

- [ ] questioning the business benefit of **punishing** those who get bad results

- [ ] weighing the negative impact of mistakes against the **learning and development** they can bring.

It's important to remember that none of this means ignoring poor results or mistakes. Financial loss or commercial reverses are bad for business. But failing to learn can be worse. The focus of management has to be the future, and what can be learned from the present and past to help shape the future. By focusing on learning and better decision making, the business is doing everything it can to do to avoid bad results in the future, rather than simply reflecting what has happened in the past.

Read more:

Traders: Risks, Decisions and Management in Financial Markets

by Mark Fenton-O'Creevy, Nigel Nicholson, Emma Soane and Paul Willman

Lessons for decision making

When things go wrong, an important area of learning is the decision-making process itself. With the benefit of hindsight, you can consider how effective your processes for making decisions were. Consider questions such as:

- [ ] how likely is it that you were influenced by a taken-for-granted **frame?**

- [ ] do you need to **rethink the way you regard risks** (i.e. as opportunities or threats)?

- [ ] are there any lessons in terms of the **way you regard outcomes** (i.e. as gains or losses)?

- [ ] did you identify all the **alternatives**, or has it become clear that unconsidered alternatives would have been better? how can you ensure that your future decision-making frames cover these alternatives?

- [ ] what information has come to light that could help to reduce the **subjectivity** of your probability assessments in future?

- [ ] how can **learning** be enshrined in the business and made easily available and usable for future decisions?

- [ ] are **downsides and/or upsides** in line with expectations? are there any unforeseen dimensions or knock-on effects in the outcome?

For any of these questions to be answered effectively, it's crucial that you have an objective record of your original decision-making processes.

Lessons for risk management

If a downside result of a specific, foreseen risk occurs, you will want to look at the way you analysed it and chose your response, and the effectiveness of the chosen response. Consider questions such as:

- [ ] are there any clear lessons for your estimates of **probability?** (for example, has an event that was regarded as extremely rare happened twice in a week?)

- [ ] how accurate was your assessment of **impact?**

  - [ ] was it more or less severe than anticipated?
  - [ ] did it affect areas you didn't predict?
  - [ ] did it have consequences of a different nature than those you expected?

- were the **plans and processes** made to deal with operational risks effective in practice?
  - should they be improved?
  - what alternatives are there?
- could operational problems **occur again**?
  - is the situation different now?
  - if not, how should it be changed?
- did you choose the right **response** to the risk?
  - how has it worked out in practice?
  - do you need to choose a different response in future, or just make the chosen response work better?
- if you chose to **tolerate** a risk, was this the right decision?
  - was it based on enough probability and impact information, or information of sufficient reliability?
- if you chose to try and **minimise** a risk, what effect did this have on its impact?
- can you demonstrate the link between your **decisions** and the positive **results** for the business?

- if you chose to **hedge** against a risk, how good was the hedge? how balanced were the different risks against each other?
- if you chose to **diversify** risks, was the extra effort worthwhile?
- if you chose to **concentrate** risks, was the saving in effort worth the extra exposure incurred?
- if a risk was **transferred**, did the third party accept responsibility when things went wrong?
- what **knock-on** effects are now apparent?
  - is the outcome fully known (or knowable), or is it still unfolding?
  - what new risks have arisen?
  - what new decisions now need to be taken?

Collective learning

Unless you have successfully eliminated a risk, there is always a probability, however small, that negative outcomes will happen. The impact can range from the highly specific and individual (such as personal injury) to the general and communal (damage to the reputation of the business). Any negative consequences are regrettable, but we can make them worse if we don't learn from them.

By failing to learn the lessons of our mistakes, we allow negative outcomes to extend into the future, instead of limiting them to the present.

The learning that comes from considering the outcomes of decisions is likely to be collective rather than individual. Individuals who frequently make a large number of decisions that are similar in nature, and stay around to observe the results, are best placed to learn from them. Weather forecasters and poker players are examples of this rare breed. Managers, unfortunately, are much less likely to make frequent decisions of a similar type and be able to learn from them.

In business, individuals are likely to move on, get promoted or retire before the consequences of their most significant decisions play themselves out to a conclusion. This makes it vital to embed the learning from major decisions in the organisation, rather than leaving it to individuals:

- ☐ **record** the information that supports decisions

- ☐ document the **decision making process**

- ☐ document **responses** to problems arising

- ☐ **share** information between decision makers.

Measures like these help to prevent information about how decisions were taken from being lost when the decision makers leave the company. Losing such information could potentially pose a major strategic risk to the organisation, since it could result in big mistakes being made again and again.

The recording of information about decisions needn't be a huge undertaking. Even brief notes on how a decision was taken can be illuminating when returned to at a later date. As we've seen, people have a strong tendency to 'edit' their memories to fit their own perspectives.

The smart organisation

Consultants and researchers David and Jim Matheson identify research and development (R&D) as a key area of decision making for business success. R&D decisions affect any areas where innovation (rather than improvement) is required. This principally means creating and marketing new products and services, but also includes designing the new processes and systems that will make them possible. 'Processes' could mean manufacturing processes, but it could also refer to strategically critical aspects of the business, such as its decision making processes.

Essentially, R&D is about ensuring that the business moves forward. As we have seen, potential strategic risk downsides include failing to innovate, failing to achieve renewal, or putting processes in place that fail to allow for the right kind of development.

The Mathesons suggest three levels of 'smart' R&D:

☐ **technology strategy:**

   ◻ how will you support existing products, generate new ones, and develop radically new ones?
   ◻ will technology be developed or supplied from inside or outside the business?
   ◻ what skills are required?

☐ **portfolio strategy:**

   ◻ which R&D projects will be funded?
   ◻ which will not?
   ◻ how will resources be allocated so that they provide the best R&D value?
   ◻ how will you balance short-term business needs with long-term renewal?

☐ **project strategy:**

   ◻ how will you ensure that each individual project delivers maximum value?
   ◻ how could commercial concerns (as well as technical, budget and timescale issues) be brought in?

They also propose nine principles of smart R&D, or the attributes that businesses need in order to be capable of making strategic decisions:

☐ **value creation culture:** the business has a purpose that everyone understands; this purpose is the test of whether strategies and actions will deliver value for the business and its customers

☐ **creating alternatives:** for each decision, there must be a good set of competing alternatives; these must be created if they don't exist or aren't apparent, and carefully evaluated

☐ **continual learning:** change is certain, and everyone must learn from new situations and information rather than feeling threatened by it

- **embracing uncertainty:** since there are no facts about the future, everyone must learn to live with and recognise uncertainty, measure and evaluate it, and understand what they are doing

- **outside-in strategic perspective:** rather than thinking about where the business is and then where it should be going (inside-out), consider the big picture first and work back to the business (outside-in)

- **systems thinking:** use tools and techniques (such as the decision tree) to simplify the complexities involved in strategic decisions as far as possible and enable insights (but not so far that objectivity is lost)

- **open information flow:** any type of information may be important, so information needs to flow, unrestricted, to all parts of the business; the habit of hoarding information as a source of power must be driven out

- **alignment and empowerment:** rather than micro-managing every action through 'command and control' systems, aim to involve people in decision making through participation, while building alignment through common understanding of goals

- **disciplined decision making:** build processes that recognise the need for strategic decisions to be made before it's too late; then apply systematic, disciplined processes to making those decisions.

Read more :
The Smart Organization
by David and Jim Matheson

Moving forward

Decision making is focused on the future. It is always forward-looking. All actions in business should be focused on what is to come: on realising positive future outcomes and avoiding negative ones.

Better risk management and decision making are means to this end; they are tools to help you achieve your goals by looking forward, not back.

At the highest level, better decision making means better strategic direction for the business. Strategy is about finding new answers the question 'what shall we do?' By enhancing your understanding of risk, you can be as sure as possible that the answers you find will take the business forward to a brighter future.

We hope you will be able to use the learning from this book to help you move forward and achieve positive outcomes by taking decisions and managing risks more effectively.

Looking back:

Key ideas from this chapter

- ☐ We make mistakes because our brains are not suited to the processes of rational decision making.

- ☐ If errors happen, we need to ensure that they have some positive impact: we need to learn from them.

- ☐ Although blame is a natural reaction, it benefits the business to create a no-blame culture.

- ☐ A no-blame culture implies that those who get bad results, but make decisions in the right way, should be rewarded.

- ☐ The smart organisation builds up its collective learning and decision-making ability to ensure a brighter future.

Index:

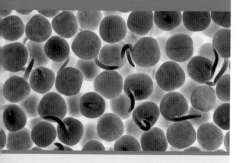